# Think It, Show It Mathematics

Strategies for Explaining Thinking

**Author**

Gregory A. Denman, M.A...

**Foreword by**

Linda Dacey, Ed.D.

D1411346

SHELL EDUCATION

## Publishing Credits

Dona Herweck Rice, *Editor-in-Chief*; Robin Erickson, *Production Director*;
Lee Aucoin, *Creative Director*; Timothy J. Bradley, *Illustration Manager*;
Sara Johnson, M.S.Ed., *Editorial Director*; Grace Alba, *Designer*;
Maribel Rendón, M.A.Ed., *Associate Eduation Editor*; Corinne Burton, M.A.Ed., *Publisher*

## Shell Education

5301 Oceanus Drive
Huntington Beach, CA 92649-1030
http://www.shelleducation.com

**ISBN 978-1-4258-1051-1**

© 2013 Shell Education Publishing, Inc.

# Table of Contents

# Acknowledgements

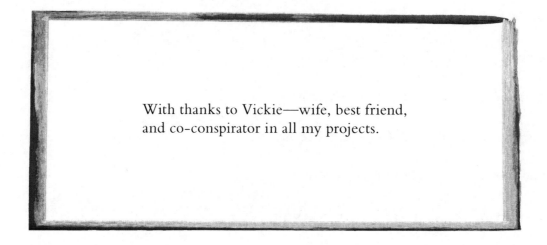

With thanks to Vickie—wife, best friend, and co-conspirator in all my projects.

# Foreword

Years ago when I was teaching fourth grade, I realized that it was possible, sometimes, to feel as if I had a lens that allowed me to see into a student's brain and realize preferred representations, misconceptions, partial ideas, and clear thinking. It was a joy to discover this possibility. The same is true now that I am teaching at the college level. Gaining access to students' thinking so that I might further facilitate their learning is, for me, the essence of teaching.

When I work with teachers, I often ask them to share a classroom set of student papers with me. When I look at responses to a mathematical problem, I learn much about the teachers' expectations for mathematical thinking and communication. It is immediately clear which teachers have found some ways to support their students' ability to explain their thinking and which have not. In *Think It, Show It Mathematics: Strategies for Demonstrating Knowledge*, Gregory Denman has provided us all with the tools we need to help students make their mathematical thinking visible.

In this book, you will find step-by-step strategies for developing students' ability to write about mathematics, beginning with structured frames that scaffold learning and moving to examples of writing that invite students to elaborate in creative ways. Most importantly, the author has provided readers with mentor texts, rubrics, and student exemplars as well as ways to use student writing to inform our instructional decisions.

The *Common Core State Standards* make it clear that students must be able to understand and communicate mathematical ideas as well as gain procedural expertise. Most importantly, the Core's *Standards for Mathematical Practice* identify the processes and practices of mathematically proficient students. Briefly, these practices highlight the need for students to make sense, reason, model, use appropriate tools, attend to precision, look for and use structure, and look for and use regularity in repeated reasoning. All students are expected to develop these abilities and will be held accountable on high-stakes tests. To meet such goals, it is critical that teachers and peers have access to students' thinking. Fortunately, Gregory Denman has many strategies for us!

—Linda Dacey, Ed.D.
Professor of Education and Mathematics
Lesley University

# Introduction

Although I was unaware of it at the time, the catalyst for the development of the activities and strategies described in this book dates back to the fall of 1999. In my home state of Colorado, that time period saw the inception of the math assessment component of the state-mandated yearly *Colorado Student Assessment Program.* Colorado public school fifth graders were tested, for the first time, in mathematics. There was much apprehension about their students' performance on the fall assessment.

When the scores were released, the results were more disappointing than had been anticipated. Fifty percent of Colorado's fifth graders had not scored as proficient. The newspaper headlines left nothing to the public's imagination. Three of the largest newspapers in the state ran these front-page proclamations the day after the results were released:

> *Half of 5th-Graders Fail Math Test*
> Rocky Mountain News, March 3, 2000
>
> *The Math Challenge: More Than Half in Test Fall Short*
> Denver Post, March 3, 2000
>
> *Half of Fifth Graders Mastering Math*
> Pueblo Chieftain, March 3, 2000

Unfortunately, that spring, the Colorado eighth graders didn't fare much better. When districts across the state started analyzing the data from the tests, they identified a persistent weakness with the written or "constructed responses" required of students. Our fifth and eighth graders demonstrated significant difficulty in communicating problem-solving procedures and their mathematical reasoning in written form.

What we saw in Colorado was not unique to students in the "Mile High State." It was mirrored across the country. Since then, more evidence of our students not only struggling with math literacy but also lagging behind other nations has been documented. The National Mathematics Advisory Panel's final report, *Foundations for Success,* cited a 2007 study that revealed that 15-year-olds in the United States ranked 25th among their peers in 30 developed nations in math literacy and problem solving.

Simply put, our students struggle with communicating their mathematical reasoning in a verbal or written form—not to mention a resistance when asked to do so. *If I got the answer correct, why do I have to explain how I got it?* is a typical response. As a result, a number of schools began to ask me to work with their students on the writing required in both the language arts and the written portions of the math test. And now, with the advent of the *Common Core State Standards,* I continue to refine the work that I do with teachers and students in order to meet those objectives. *Think It, Show It Mathematics: Strategies for Explaining Thinking,* along with its materials, is a result of my work and research with teachers and students in an effort to help all students better demonstrate their mathematical understandings through writing and discussion.

Through this work, I have found ways to merge practical and dependable writing strategies with ongoing day-to-day mathematics instruction. For example, students use "framed paragraphs" to facilitate formulas for a written explanation of the solving of a word problem and thereby learn how writing in mathematics needs to be read and sound. The language of these "mathematical framed paragraphs" later functions as mental templates that students can fall back on, as needed, as they mature and begin working with more challenging problems. By becoming proficient with these types of paragraphs, students can internalize the sound and structure of a basic math narrative.

Below is a third-grade written explanation sample. For readability purposes, students' spelling errors have been corrected throughout the book.

> To solve the problem, I first added the 9 absent boys and the 3 absent girls and found 12 students. After that, I subtracted the 12 students from the 23 students that were in class and found 11 students. Therefore, I know Alicia's class had only 11 students left.
>
> 3rd Grade Student

Another example is using the method of writing a mathematical procedural text employing "what" and "why" statements: operations and corresponding reasons. "What" statements are statements of what mathematical operations students need to do to solve the problem, and "why" statements are statements explaining why they need to use these operations with specific references to contextual details found in the stated problem. Included with these explanations are "why" words *(since* and *because)* along with a handful of good procedural transition or sequence words *(to start with, first, then, after that, second, etc.),* and the perfect wording to start a concluding sentence *(Therefore, I know):*

In order for me to solve this problem, I first (*transition word*) multiplied 4 times $3.25 (*what statement*) because (*why word*) I needed to know how much money Jessica had earned each day for the 4 hours she babysat (*why statement*). I found she earned $13.00 a day. Since (*why word*) Jessica worked 3 days a week (*why statement*), I multiplied 3 times the $13.00 she earned each day (*what statement*). I found that equaled $39.00. Therefore, I know that Jessica had earned a total of $39.00 each week babysitting (*concluding sentence*).

5th Grade Student

Incorporated in the activity sheets students use with this strategy are "problem-solving questions" for students to address before attempting to map out the steps they need to follow in solving the problem:

- What is happening in the problem?
- What do I know?
- What is my data?
- What don't I know?
- What is the problem asking me to find out?
- What will my answer tell me?

These questions align with the goals of the *Common Core State Standards for Mathematics:* Practice Standard 1: Make Sense of Problems and Persevere in Solving Them.

> "Mathematically proficient students start by explaining to themselves the meaning of a problem and looking for entry points to its solution. They analyze givens, constraints, relationships, and goals. They make conjectures about the form and meaning of the solution and plan a solution pathway rather than simply jumping into a solution attempt."

*Common Core State Standards for Mathematics* 2010, 6

Using "what" and "why statements" along with "why" words and "transition/sequence words" helps students learn to strategically construct a coherent and logical explanation of a mathematical process. If students know the math, if they can develop a solution using convincing mathematical reasoning, then they can be taught how to clearly communicate this understanding in words. The process used to teach these strategies is the basis of this book.

Mathematics teachers, like classroom teachers in all subject areas, have full, if not, filled-beyond-capacity, instructional plates. Therefore, the strategies presented in this book can easily be integrated into any classroom, with any story or word problem, and with any curriculum that teachers are using.

Working with so many students and teachers during the development of these strategies and materials has been rewarding and edifying. The desire of teachers to have practical and effective methods to help their students perform better has forced me, as well as the teachers I worked with, to refine the material that is presented in this book. Classroom teachers, mathematics specialists, and curriculum directors as well as university instructors have been continually questioned about the effectiveness of the material. They have helped tremendously by pointing out where a different wording might be used or how a certain format might be confusing to a certain age group. I am so very grateful. With their insights, the process described in this book has enabled a great many students across the country to gain confidence and proficiency when asked to explain their mathematical thinking.

—Greg

# Why Write in Mathematics?

The *Common Core State Standards* insist that instruction in reading, writing, speaking, and language be a shared responsibility within the school.

Let's start by posing a question I ask of teachers when conducting an in-service on the math writing process: If there weren't a test that required students to explain their mathematical thinking, would we be teaching it in our classrooms?

To answer this, we need to briefly examine the changes that have occurred in the curriculum of mathematics over the last three decades.

The last 30 years have seen a gradual but tremendous change in the instruction of mathematics. It has become much more than the traditional computation skills—adding, subtracting, dividing, working with fractions and percentages, etc. As we make our way into the challenges of today's mathematically and technologically sophisticated world, students need not only to be able to solve problems using computation but also to reason mathematically and use that same reasoning capacity in tackling real-life situations that involve mathematics. This idea is foundational in the *Common Core State Standards in Mathematics* (2010).

Much of the change and reprioritizing that we are presently seeing with the instruction of mathematics through the *Common Core State Standards* has been as a result of the original vision, work, and efforts of the *National Council of Teachers of Mathematics* (NCTM 2000). *The Standards for Mathematical Practice* with the *Common Core* describe varieties of expertise that mathematics educators at all levels should seek to develop in their students. These practices rest on important processes and proficiencies with longstanding importance in mathematics education. The first of these are the NCTM process standards of problem solving, reasoning and proof, communication, representation, and connections (2000, 6).

NCTM's Five Process Standards focus the instruction of mathematics around the activities, processes, and practice with problem-solving skills—not simply finding the right answer to a specific problem. In addition to critical computational skills, students need to be able to use mathematical reasoning in determining whether their answers or solutions make sense. Students must articulate a rationale and be able to evaluate an alternative approach(es). The *Common Core State Standards for Mathematics* states that "mathematically proficient students justify their conclusions, communicate them to others, and respond to the arguments of others" (2010, 6). Explaining their solution and reasoning and defending or justifying their approach with mathematical evidence becomes an integral part of the problem-solving process. This, of course, leads the student-learner into the need for precise skills in both verbal and written communication. In the math classroom of the 21st century, students must be able to verbalize and write coherently about complex mathematical ideas in the language of mathematics.

Writing has been referred to as "thinking made visible." Indeed, the objective of the *Common Core State Standards for Mathematics* is that our students learn to communicate mathematically by correctly using the appropriate symbols, vocabulary, and labeling. The standards prepare students to:

- organize and consolidate their mathematical thinking through communication.

- communicate their mathematical thinking coherently and clearly to peers, teachers, and others.

- analyze and evaluate the mathematical thinking and strategies of others.

- use the language of mathematics to express mathematical ideas precisely.

Given the principles, processes, and standards articulated by the *Common Core State Standards*, the goals and implementation of state assessment tests, and the never-ending challenges of precious available instructional time that every teacher faces, let's examine the benefits of mathematical writing in the classroom for both students and their teachers.

## Thinking Made Visible

This book emphasizes that writing in mathematics offers numerous benefits, as listed below:

### Provides teachers with insight into

- thought processes underlying students' problem-solving skills

- students' understanding of mathematical principles in the context of real-life situations

- the academic strengths and weaknesses of their students in order to more accurately identify and align instruction and to give students specific feedback

### Provides students with opportunities to

- demonstrate their competencies and understanding of mathematical principles

- recognize their own mistakes and/or faulty mathematical reasoning

- clarify and refine their thinking

- hear and evaluate alternative problem-solving strategies

- see how they can use and transfer skills from one subject area to another (language arts to math)

Here is a sample word problem that can help illustrate these benefits.

> Todd and his parents decide to turn the spare bedroom in their house into a really cool game room. It will not only be a place where Todd can play games on his computer and watch TV and movies, but it will also have a foosball table for him and his friends to enjoy. They decide they will need to carpet exactly half of the room. If the bedroom is 18 feet by 14 feet, how many square feet of carpet will Todd's parents need to buy? Explain how you found your answer.

Below and on the next page are three samples of fourth-grade written explanations.

### Student Sample 1

To start with, I multiplied 14 feet by 18 feet because I need to know the area of the room. I found 252 square feet. Second, I took the 252 square feet and divided it by two because Todd's parents were only going to carpet half of the room. I found 126 square feet. Therefore, I know that they will need to buy 126 square feet of carpet.

### Student Sample 2

To start with, I multiplied 14 feet by 18 feet because to find area you multiply length by width. I found 252 square feet. Next ,I divided the 252 square feet by 2 because they wanted to carpet only half of the game room, and I found 126 square feet. Therefore, I know that Todd's parents needed 126 square feet of carpet for the room.

4th Grade Students

> ## Student Sample 3
>
> First, I multiplied 18 feet by 14 feet because I needed to find the area of the game room. I found 252 square feet. Then, I divided the 252 square feet by 2 because only half of the game room would be carpeted. I found 126. Therefore, I know that Todd's parents will need 126 square feet of carpet unless they sell the house or a natural disaster hits!
>
> 4th Grade Student

Each of these students obviously wrote a solid (and in one case clever) response. Not only did they demonstrate a conceptual understanding (difference between perimeter and area, the operation necessary to determine area, and the fact that division of a number by two equals one half of the number), but they also did each calculation correctly at the operational level. The sequenced and logical construction of their writing demonstrated successfully integrated writing skills. As suggested earlier, these samples confirm that if students know the math and use mathematical reasoning, they can be taught how to communicate that understanding with words.

Beyond just getting a "correct" answer, it can be argued that there is power (and magic) in the pure satisfaction of a correct and logically presented mathematical explanation. By having them explain their mathematical process, students have been asked to wrestle with the construction and articulation of the thinking behind their answers, and in the examples of these students, they have done just that. It's certain that when students orally share their written responses in class, especially those who have written like the sampled students above, they read with a confidence that cries out: *I know what I am doing and how to do it!* It can be thought of as mathematically-empowered students in the making. Another student, however, addressing the same math problem did not fare so well.

> ## Student Sample 4
>
> Since they are only carpeting half of the room, I cut the length and width in half and then multiplied them together. I found 63 square feet. Therefore, I know that they will need 63 square feet of carpet.
>
> 4th Grade Student

At this point, the student was confused and not sure where he had gone wrong, so I simply asked him to draw the shape of the room to explain what he had done as the first step of his written response.

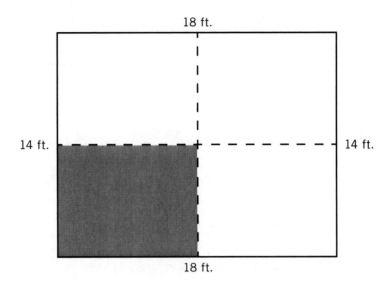

You could have heard the *"Ah…I get it!"* all the way down the hall when he discovered *on his own* that by cutting both the length and the width in half and then multiplying them, he was finding only one-fourth of the area of the room. He could now easily revise his written answer.

At the same time, another student, knowing that he was encouraged to visualize and sketch out the details of the problem the class is working on, did just that and produced an alternative solution.

---

### Student Sample 5

To solve the problem, I first drew the 14 ft. by 18 ft. game room and decided to cut it in half down the middle. This gave me a length of 9 ft. So, I multiplied 14 ft. by 9 ft. and found an area of 126 square feet. Therefore, I know that Todd's game room will need 126 square feet of carpet.

4th Grade Student

---

With this student's written explanation, the entire class was able to hear and evaluate another way to solve the problem.

In order for students to progress toward mastering the skill of communicating in mathematics, they need as much specific individual feedback as possible on what they produce. Consider, for example, the work of Student 6.

**Student Sample 6**

First, I multiplied 14 by 18 and I found 252, and it is the area of the room. Then, I divided 2 by 252 and I found 126, and that is half of the room. Therefore, I know that is half the room.

4th Grade Student

The criteria for the nine-point rubric *Explaining Your Math Thinking in Words* is used (presented in greater detail later in the book) as a reference. See Figure 1.1.

**Figure 1.1** Explaining Your Math Thinking in Words

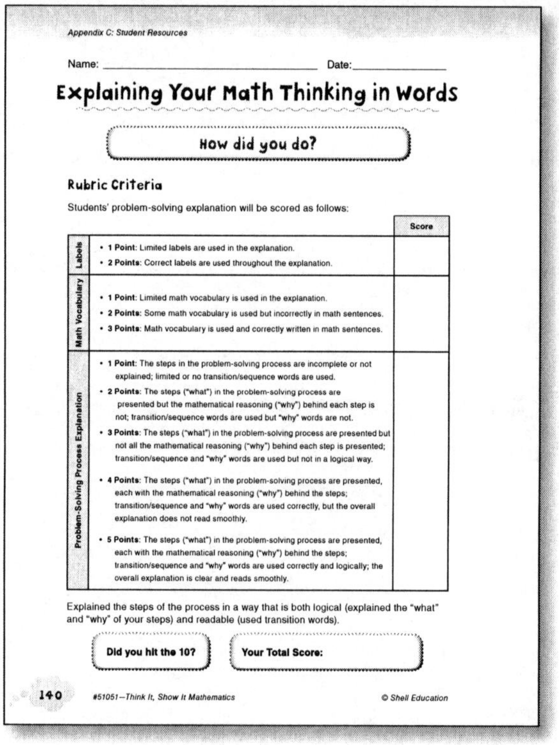

*Appendix C: Student Resources*

Name: ______________________ Date: __________

**Explaining Your Math Thinking in Words**

**How did you do?**

**Rubric Criteria**

Students' problem-solving explanation will be scored as follows:

| | | Score |
|---|---|---|
| Labels | • **1 Point**: Limited labels are used in the explanation.<br>• **2 Points**: Correct labels are used throughout the explanation. | |
| Math Vocabulary | • **1 Point**: Limited math vocabulary is used in the explanation.<br>• **2 Points**: Some math vocabulary is used but incorrectly in math sentences.<br>• **3 Points**: Math vocabulary is used and correctly written in math sentences. | |
| Problem-Solving Process Explanation | • **1 Point**: The steps in the problem-solving process are incomplete or not explained; limited or no transition/sequence words are used.<br>• **2 Points**: The steps ("what") in the problem-solving process are presented but the mathematical reasoning ("why") behind each step is not; transition/sequence words are used but "why" words are not.<br>• **3 Points**: The steps ("what") in the problem-solving process are presented but not all the mathematical reasoning ("why") behind each step is presented; transition/sequence and "why" words are used but not in a logical way.<br>• **4 Points**: The steps ("what") in the problem-solving process are presented, each with the mathematical reasoning ("why") behind the steps; transition/sequence and "why" words are used correctly, but the overall explanation does not read smoothly.<br>• **5 Points**: The steps ("what") in the problem-solving process are presented, each with the mathematical reasoning ("why") behind the steps; transition/sequence and "why" words are used correctly and logically; the overall explanation is clear and reads smoothly. | |

Explained the steps of the process in a way that is both logical (explained the "what" and "why" of your steps) and readable (used transition words).

**Did you hit the 10?** **Your Total Score:**

140 *#51051—Think It, Show It Mathematics* *© Shell Education*

Using the rubric criteria as a guide, the teacher or members of a cooperative learning group, could conference with students to give them thorough feedback to take steps toward mastering the math explanation. It should be pointed out that the student knew how to solve the problem and had calculated correctly. She used transition words (*first, then,* and *therefore*) to sequence the steps of her explanation. The student would then have to be shown how points were lost for failing to use labels *(14 what? 18 what?).* Further, the student did not write the division operation in a correct math sentence *(2 by 252).* We would need to write the operation as a number sentence to work on that. The conference would then conclude by having the student reread the original word problem to determine exactly what the answer should tell us *(how many square feet of carpet Todd's parents will need, not the size of half the room),* reminding the student that the concluding sentence in a math explanation must always answer exactly what the problem is asking.

Finally, by going through the entire class's written responses from the day's work, it was decided that there were four mini-lessons to be conducted that week:

- Demonstrate how including labels throughout their answers helps avoid confusion.

- Use a consistent tense (multiplied, found, needed, divided, etc.) in the written paragraph by using some examples from students' work.

- Emphasize how helpful it can be to visualize and sketch out a problem before attempting to solve it.

- Stress how important it is to always reread written answers quietly to ourselves to see if they make sense or if any words were inadvertently left out.

Writing narratives in mathematics give students the opportunity to become aware of their thinking process while problem solving. Students are able to write coherent and logical explanations of their problem-solving process. Additionally, students are afforded the opportunity to reduce or eliminate mistakes. By explaining their thought processes, students are held accountable for their work while furthering their mathematical knowledge.

#51051—Think It, Show It Mathematics

# One- and Two-Step Problems

Problem solving in mathematics forms a foundation for student success and "is not only a goal of learning mathematics but also a major means of doing so" (NCTM 2000, 4). According to the *Common Core State Standards*, students must be able to apply mathematics to solve problems that occur in everyday life as well as explain their thinking and communicate their solution (2010). By solving mathematical problems, students experience opportunities to think mathematically, persevere in solutions, develop curiosity and confidence, and make connections to mathematics and the real world (NCTM 2000). As suggested in the opening chapter, problem solving allows teachers to build mathematically empowered students and requires students to think critically and creatively in order to arrive at solutions.

This level of thinking, problem solving, and mathematical competence is even more critical today with an increasing number of students using calculators. As essential tools in our classrooms and lives, calculators serve us by giving us right answers, but reliance on them can allow students to circumvent an understanding of the mathematical principles involved with a given situation.

I am reminded of my attempt to buy a sweater at a department store awhile back. It was a $50 sweater reduced by 20 percent. A great deal! So I picked up the sweater and headed to a counter. Unfortunately, the clerk there had misplaced her calculator and was flustered. "You'll need to go to the other counter," she apologized. I looked and saw a line of six or seven people. Not wanting to deal with a long wait, I simply told the clerk that 20 percent of $50.00 is $10.00 and if we subtracted that from the $50.00, the sweater would cost $40.00. "So just key $40.00 into your register and figure the tax and I'll be on my way," I suggested. But the clerk still insisted that she needed her calculator. "It's not that I don't trust you," she confessed, "but I always use my calculator." Finally, she had an idea and picked up her telephone, called another clerk, and explained, word-for-word, exactly what keys to press on her calculator, and they found—lo and behold—that with the 20 percent discount, the sweater would only cost $40.00.

I am not being terribly critical of the clerk (trust me—I rely heavily on my calculator when averaging grades, balancing my check book, and doing taxes!). It does, however, illustrate how important it is for students to go beyond the computations afforded by a calculator to understanding the mathematical processes and principles underlying what they key into their calculators. In the case of my department store clerk, it was to understand the function of percentages in determining the price of a discounted sweater.

Another case in point returns us to the fourth-grade students who were working with the problem of Todd and the carpeting of his game room that I discussed in the first chapter. Earlier in the year, these same students had been given activity sheets on which they practiced calculating perimeters and areas that were presented pictorially. But later in the year some of them were baffled when the two mathematical tasks were placed side-by-side in the real-life context of Todd and the square feet of carpet required for his game room. Our students need to become skilled in addressing and understanding word problems as they might be encountered in everyday life.

## Addressing Word Problems

We start teaching students how to explain their mathematical thinking by showing them how to first systematically address word problems. The process follows these steps:

### Read → Decide → Estimate → Work → Explain

**1. Read the Problem**

- What is happening in the problem?
- What do I know?
- What don't I know?
- What is the problem asking me to find out?

**2. Decide**

- What operation(s) will I need to do to solve the problem?
- What strategy will I use to solve the problem?

**3. Make an Estimation**

- What is a reasonable answer?

**4. Work the Problem**

- Check my work.

**5. Explain My Math Thinking in Writing**

The first step with any word problem is to establish what is happening. The *Common Core State Standards for Mathematics* describes mathematically proficient students as ones who "start by explaining to themselves the meaning of a problem" (2010, 6). Students should be regularly asked to explain in their own words what is happening in a given problem. A fun yet effective way to do this is to have students reframe what is happening as if they were telling it as a story by starting with the words *once upon a time*. Here is a student example based on the following word problem:

> Farmer Arturo had 165 cows in his pasture. One night, some pranksters opened his gate, and 39 cows wandered out into his neighbor's pasture. How many cows does Farmer Arturo have left in his own pasture? Explain how you found your solution.

> Once upon a time, there was a farmer named Farmer Arturo who had 165 cows in his pasture. But one day, some guys came in and let 39 of his cows out of his pasture. Farmer Arturo was so sad! He wanted to know how many of his cows he had left.
>
> 3rd Grade Student

Students are then asked to share their "stories" with their learning partners or to share and listen to one another in cooperative learning groups. Students are also encouraged to visualize the problem's situation and make a drawing or sketch to represent the problem situation. This is important because students often want to read problems as quickly as they can and jump immediately into doing the calculation. The desired result is "I'm the first one done!" being loudly announced as their arms and pencils are launched straight up into the air. This "being-done-first" mindset, of course, is common among many students. It is true that in the early grades, many students often are able to correctly solve some problems without careful and analytical reading. However, as they progress into more difficult and multifaceted mathematics, this assuredly will not continue to be the case. Students need to develop a mathematical "habit of thought" when working with word problems by always explaining to themselves what is happening in the problem.

Fundamental in the careful reading of a word problem in order to solve it is the determination of the essential information. They are the "givens" or "what do I know?" Along with "what do I know," students need to address "what don't I know." Determining this often involves the identification of the words.

It is important to note that not all word problems have specific clue (key) words such as these:

- How many altogether?
- How many in total?
- How many in all?

- How many fewer?
- How many would be left?
- What would remain?

Also in the wording of some problems, clue words can actually be misleading. Given this, some researchers have cautioned against using them as a strategy in the analysis of a word problem (Van DeWalle, 2009). However, many core curriculums refer to clue/key words, and students are asked to identify them when they can but only as one of the many available strategies they can use in understanding what the problem is asking. Students need to carefully read the problem in order to make sense of it. A final key element in this step is for students to circle the key number facts in the problem (i.e., *165 cows and 39 cows*) and underline the problem being asked (i.e., *How many cows does Farmer Arturo have left in his own pasture?*)

Step two asks students to determine what strategy or mathematical operation is needed to solve the problem. Some of these strategies include:

- draw a picture
- work backwards
- create a table
- find a pattern
- create a diagram

- create a list
- guess and check
- write an equation/number sentence
- use simpler numbers

Many times, drawing a picture or diagram, making a list, working a simpler version of the problem, or using patterns is the perfect strategy. As students continue working and growing in mathematics, they will become more comfortable in finding a workable way to solve a problem, or as articulated in the *Common Core State Standards for Mathematics*, "plan a solution pathway" (2010, 6). Students will discover that there may be more than one "pathway" that will lead to a correct solution. They should, therefore, start at an early age identifying and stating the strategies or pathways necessary to solve their problems. By explicitly employing problem-solving strategies and writing and discussing those strategies, students make clear the process they are following and provide teachers a window into their thinking. This is important as students progress into more difficult mathematics in order to know whether students are truly gaining conceptual understanding or simply have a rote procedural understanding of the problem (Gojak 2011).

Step three involves making an estimation to find a reasonable answer to check the final solution against. This is an important step in the process in order to help students gauge whether they are on the right track once they have completed the problem. If their estimation is way off from their final answer, students should go back and check their work in order to see if they made a calculation or other mathematical error. This is especially important when students are using calculators. Students often think of calculators as always displaying correct answers. And although a calculator will always compute correctly, students need to remember that they could have made a mistake entering the numbers or the operations, and they should check their final answer against their estimation. For example, although the calculator may display 42, that answer is unreasonable as the average points scored by a team were 25, 17, 34, and 43 points.

A simple way to work with estimations is to explain that when performing calculations, estimation is substituting numbers that we can easily add in our heads, or at least with minimal effort using paper and pencil, to give us a reasonable answer. Very often, this involves rounding and thinking in sets of easy-to-calculate numbers such as fives, tens, and hundreds. Another way to have students think about calculation estimations is to refer to them as "pre-answers."

In the broader picture, the ongoing practice of making estimations allows us to circumvent possible headaches in our day-to-day lives. For example, if I am picking up fencing material to build a dog run in my backyard and know that the area measures 9 feet by 13 feet, I would first round 9 to 10 and 13 to 15. That way I can go to the hardware store having mentally calculated that 10 and 10 equals 20, and that 15 and 15 equals 30, and finally that 20 plus 30 makes 50. Therefore, 50 feet of fence is certainly going to work. Knowing this, I would not have the hassle of having to return to the store a couple of hours later to purchase another 10-foot roll because I arbitrarily guessed 40 feet would be enough. Or if I am having my son run to the grocery store to pick up three items, I can estimate how much they will cost and give him the right amount of money so he doesn't have to come back complaining that he didn't have enough and grumbling about having to make a second trip back to the store.

At this point, let's turn our attention to the last two steps of the process: working the actual problem and then explaining their problem-solving steps in words. Here, students use a "framed paragraph" in order to support the language necessary to draw a conclusion about the mathematical processes used to find and clearly communicate the solution.

## One-Step Word Problems

One-step word problems involve scenarios in which only one calculation is needed in order to arrive at the solution. The *One-Step Problems* activity sheet pictured in Figure 2.1 should be used when students are working with single-step math problems. In order to be truly successful with this process, students need a framework to support the problem-solving steps and the language needed to clearly communicate their solution and conclusions. Not only is it important to provide guidance for students to frame the mathematics but also by using these framed paragraphs, students hear how writing in math "sounds." Through repeated exposure to writing and hearing these math narratives, students internalize their linguistic pattern.

**Figure 2.1** One-Step Problems

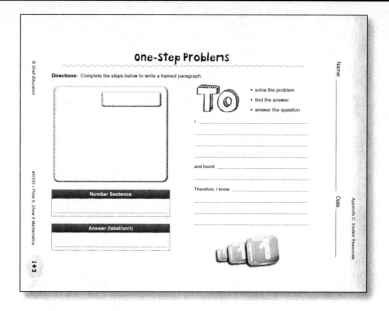

Students start on the left side of the sheet with the large blank work area. They are to record the label or unit from the problem at the top of the space in the rectangle provided (e.g., puppies, basketballs, or cows). They then work the problem they identified in step two using whatever strategy they have chosen to solve the problem.

## Try It!

Some teachers have enlarged the *One-Step Problems* activity sheet included with this book and laminated it so that students can draw using an overhead pen or perhaps work with manipulatives or number strips in the actual work area on the sheet and then complete it.

The next step is for them to write a number sentence in the correct box for the mathematical operation that they performed. This is completed during step 4 of the problem-solving process previously discussed. A correctly constructed number sentence will help them express it correctly with words in their subsequent written paragraph. For example, if they correctly write the number sentence as *165 − 39 = 126*, they more likely will write out *165 minus 39 equals 126* as opposed to reversing the minuend and subtrahend (*39 minus 165*).

Writing number sentences correctly, however, is predicated on two pieces of critical mathematical knowledge (Figure 2.2):

- Conceptual knowledge of what the mathematical operation means

- Symbolic knowledge of what math symbols ( =, +, −, ×, ÷) represent in the expression of a number sentence

Working at the conceptual knowledge, it is generally helpful to go back to "models" of subtraction *(using drawings, physical manipulatives, number strips or number patterns, etc.)* to help the student construct an understanding of what subtraction is.

**Figure 2.2** Math Symbols and Math Words

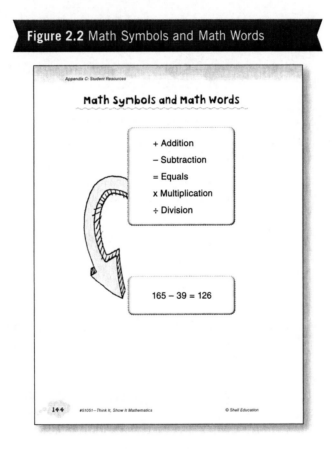

For struggling students, some teachers have found it helpful to scaffold their learning by drawing squares and circles on the Number Sentence rectangle on the *One-Step Problems* activity sheet. These guide students in writing their number sentences. Students know that numbers are written in the squares and symbols in the circles. See Figure 2.3 for a visual reference of this guide.

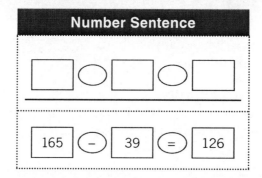

**Figure 2.3** Number Sentence Scaffold

Finally, from the correctly constructed number sentence, students write the answer to the problem with its label or unit in the Answer (label/unit) box. This is also completed during step 4 of the problem-solving process previously discussed. Students are now ready to move to the right side of the sheet for the written explanations of their mathematical work. This is part of step 5 in the problem-solving process. Here, students complete the framed paragraph on the sheet by first selecting and circling one of the phrases to continue the sentence: To _____

- solve the problem

- find the answer

- answer the question

All of these phrases will work perfectly in any math narrative, but by choosing, using, and hearing different ones, students not only learn a variety of ways to begin their paragraphs but also have the satisfaction of choosing phrases on their own.

Then, referring to the left side of the sheet where they have written their number sentences, they write the numbers in words, and operations they performed to arrive at their solution. Here they can refer to the chart shown in Figure 2.4 to help them determine which words to use in their sentences as well as their correct spellings. They see that when we subtract, we use the math symbol for minus (–) in our number sentences but use the written words (*minus, subtracted, from,* or *take away*) when we write our explanation in words. This sentence stresses how important it is to include the labels or units not only with their final sentence but also throughout the written responses *(I subtracted 39 what? from 165 what? and found 126 what?).* It is important for students to understand that by including labels throughout the paragraphs, they demonstrate that they understand the situation presented in the original word problem.

The final sentence starts simply with "Therefore, I know" to conclude the paragraph. Students must understand that their last or concluding sentence has to directly answer the question that they underlined in the word problem. This is further detailed on page 28.

They finish their sentences, of course, by writing the solution they found in the Answer (label/unit) box. The chart shown in Figure 2.4 is helpful to display around the room at the math learning centers. Students should also keep copies of it in their math journals.

**Figure 2.4** Math Symbols and Math Words Chart

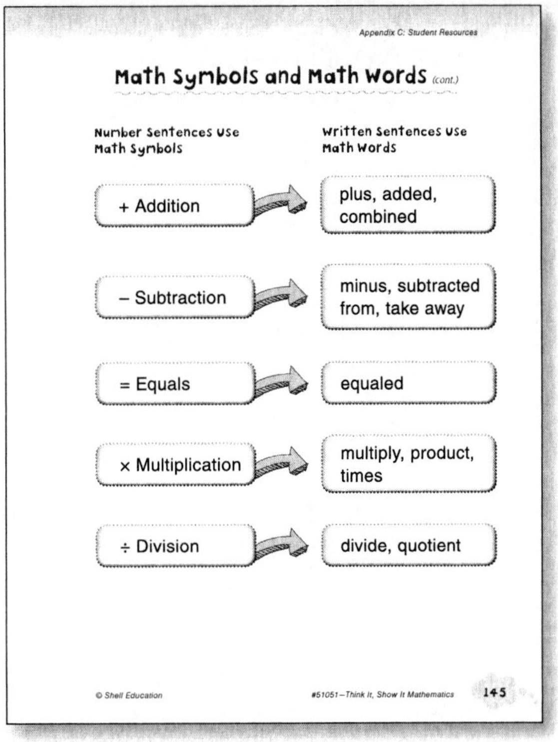

*Appendix C: Student Resources*

**Math Symbols and Math Words** *(cont.)*

| Number Sentences Use Math Symbols | Written Sentences Use Math Words |
|---|---|
| + Addition | plus, added, combined |
| − Subtraction | minus, subtracted from, take away |
| = Equals | equaled |
| × Multiplication | multiply, product, times |
| ÷ Division | divide, quotient |

© Shell Education    #51051—Think It, Show It Mathematics    **145**

Let's return to the word problem about Farmer Arturo to further investigate this four-step problem-solving process. Because the mathematics in this example is relatively simple, it is a great way to introduce the problem-solving process so that students can gain a level of proficiency with it before working with more challenging mathematical situations.

Farmer Arturo had 165 cows in his pasture. One night, some pranksters opened his gate, and 39 cows wandered out into his neighbor's pasture. How many cows does Farmer Arturo have left in his own pasture? Explain how you found your solution.

**1.** **Read the Problem**

○ What is happening in the problem?

○ What do I know?

○ What don't I know?

○ What is the problem asking me to find out?

In order to help students understand the problem, it is important to work together to answer each question in step one.

- What is happening in the problem?
  Farmer Arturo's cows have been let out of his pasture. Some are still inside his pasture, but some are in his neighbor's pasture.

- What do I know?
  Farmer Arturo started with 165 cows. There were 39 cows let out of his pasture.

- What don't I know?
  We don't know how many cows Farmer Arturo has left in his pasture.

- What is the problem asking us to find out?
  We need to find out how many cows Farmer Arturo had left in his pasture after his gate had been left open and some of his cows wandered out.

The last two questions may appear to be repetitive and essentially contain the same information, but by having students systematically address each of them, we help them refine and practice their analytical thinking and problem-solving skills. We are not solely looking for a correct figure (*126 cows*). We are looking for a correct answer in the specific context of the word problem's situation (*126 cows are left in Farmer Arturo's pasture*). This level of contextual detail helps prepare students for the more advanced problems they will encounter as they progress into the higher grades. To reinforce this, it is helpful to have students underline the question asked in each of their word problems. In this case, students would have underlined as follows: *How many cows does Farmer Arturo have left in his own pasture?*

Depending on the age of students and the level of detail desired in the math problems, an alternative version of the Farmer Arturo problem can be presented. This version provides some extra information and distractors.

Farmer Arturo is a good farmer. He and his wife live in a small farmhouse with their three children. Their pasture is lined with beautiful cottonwood trees. In his pasture, Farmer Arturo has 165 cows. He takes good care of his cows. But one day, some pranksters from the town decided to play a trick on Farmer Arturo. While he and his wife were asleep, they quietly crept up to his pasture and opened his gate. "Boy," they thought, "is Farmer Arturo in for a surprise when he gets up in the morning!" And they were right. When Farmer Arturo and his family got up the next morning, they discovered that 39 of his cows had wandered out of his pasture and into his neighbor's pasture.

How many cows does Farmer Arturo have left in his own pasture?

Discussion about this problem is very similar to what was shared regarding the simpler version; however, there should be richer discourse around what is needed and not needed in order to solve this problem.

- Important information *needed* in solving the problem:
  Farmer Arturo had 165 cows in his pasture.
  He discovered that 39 of his cows wandered into his neighbor's pasture.

- Interesting but unimportant information not needed to solve the problem:
  Farmer Arturo is a good farmer.
  He takes good care of his cows.
  He has a wife and three children.
  They live in a small farmhouse.
  His pasture is lined with cottonwood trees.

These discussions prompt students to realize that not all of the numbers presented in the problem are important to the actual solution. The fact that Farmer Arturo and his wife have three children has nothing to do with determining how many cows he has left in his pasture. In order to help students ignore the unneeded numbers, have students draw a circle around the important information necessary to solve the problem. In this problem, students would draw circles around "165 cows" and "39 cows." We are now prepared for the next step.

 **Decide**

- What operation(s) will I need to do to solve the problem?

- What strategy will I use to solve the problem?

There are many problem-solving strategies that can be used to help students solve this problem. One good visual strategy for this scenario is to draw a picture. At this point, the teacher should then work at the board or on a chart with the class, constructing a visual representation of what the process would look like (Figure 2.5).

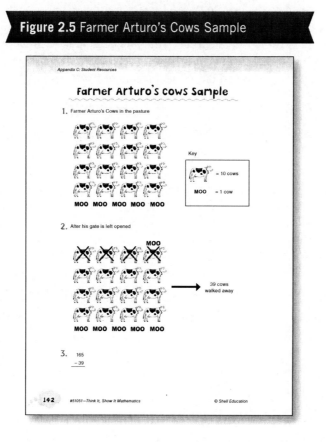

**Figure 2.5** Farmer Arturo's Cows Sample

The teacher models the creation of this drawing/diagram using the think-aloud below:

*"Okay, students, Farmer Arturo has 165 cows in his pasture. We can draw the pasture, but do you think we can actually draw 165 cows in it? Any ideas about how we can show the 165 cows? Making a key, Cindy? That's a great idea. How about using a little cow as our symbol? How many cows should each of our little cows represent? Good, Joseph, 10…that's a good strategy since we know that we can easily skip-count by tens. Now count with me and tell me how many little cows we'll need. We'll need 16 little cows, Carlos? But that only makes 160 cows. How can we show 5 more cows to make the 165? We could write the word* moo*…another wonderful idea, thank you, Liz.*

*Now we need to show that 39 cows left the pasture. The number 39 is very close to 40. If we cross out 40 cows, how many cows would we need to put back into the pasture to make sure that only 39 total are subtracted? One. That is absolutely correct, class. We can show that by writing the word* moo *one more time. Now our pasture shows how many are left."*

### 3. Make an Estimation

  ○ What is a reasonable answer?

In order to make an estimation for the solution to this problem, students only need to round one number (39) in order to have a simple calculation to work with. The think-aloud previously modeled shows the beginning of using estimation with this problem. In their heads, students should be able to calculate that 165 minus 40 equals 125 and know that the final solution should be about 125 cows.

### 4. Work the Problem

  ○ Check my work.

### 5. Explain My Math Thinking in Writing

In order to work the problem, the teacher brings students back to the original drawing. By counting the remaining cows left in the picture, students can see that there are 126 cows left in the pasture. A subtraction sentence should also be used to shows this. In order to model what was completed in the picture, students should write the sentence $165 - 40 = 125 + 1 = 126$. This shows that they first subtracted 40 cows and then added one cow back to make sure that only a total of 39 were actually taken away from the original 165 cows. They then record their final answer as *126 cows*.

At this point, students begin writing their paragraphs to explain their mathematical thinking using the scaffold provided in the *One-Step Problems* activity sheet. A student example of a completed *One-Step Problems* activity sheet (Figure 2.6) is located on the next page. Underneath is the student's final written paragraph. As an option, students rewrite their paragraphs in their math journals or on writing paper to be displayed on the classroom walls. It is important to look for many opportunities for students to read their paragraphs aloud and to hear others read theirs in order to practice verbalizing their thoughts and reinforce the precise mathematical language needed to explain the content and problem-solving process being used.

**Figure 2.6** One-Step Problems Student Sample

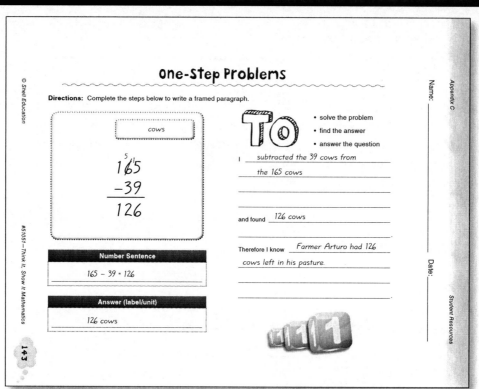

To solve the problem, I subtracted the 39 cows from the 165 cows and found 126 cows. Therefore, I know Farmer Arturo had 126 cows left in his pasture.

3rd Grade Student

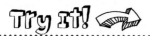

After using the *One-Step Problems* activity sheet you may want to extend your students' learning by having them take their number sentence (165 − 39 = 126) and write and illustrate their own word problems.

There are 165 second graders at Emerson Elementary School, but one day 39 of them were sick and didn't come to school. How many students were left at school that day?

3rd Grade Student

There may be some students who are not ready to work independently with the *One-Step Problems* activity sheet. They may struggle not only with the computation, but also with writing the number sentences and then transferring them into a written sentence. Figure 2.7 displays an activity sheet that can be used to give these students practice with this sequence. To use this activity sheet, students must first be provided a problem. The problem is to be worked in the first box using drawings, number strips, or manipulatives—whatever is most helpful for students—to find the answer. In box two, students record the operation as a number sentence. Finally, students take their number sentence and write it as a written sentence in box three, where they have the spelling of the words they need.

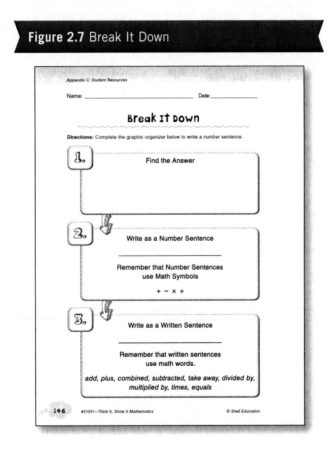

**Figure 2.7** Break It Down

Here is another example of a one-step problem solved by using the *One-Step Problems* activity sheet.

Chris wants to get cool new headbands for his three buddies to use when they play basketball at recess. He knows that each headband will cost $4.36, including tax. How much money will Chris need to buy the headbands?

> To solve the problem, $4.36 plus $4.36 plus $4.36 were added, and a total of $13.08 was found. Therefore, I know that Chris will need $13.08 to buy headbands for his three buddies.
>
> 3rd Grade Student

Between the word problem in the box and a student's written explanation just below it, much mathematical learning and demonstration of this learning has occurred.

First, of course, there is the correct computational skill of adding money (*$4.36 + $4.36 + $4.36 = $13.08*), with all that it entails (*addition facts, lining up the decimals, regrouping from the hundredths to the tenths, etc.*). Also there is the use of correct mathematical language (*using the word* [plus] *as opposed to inserting its symbol* [+]). But even before the student started the calculations, there was the actual circumstance—the context in which the problem was presented. By embedding the mathematical problem within the situation of a boy named Chris wanting to get headbands for his friends, the operation of addition was placed in a real-life scenario. The addition of money was no longer only an abstract task to be practiced and mastered, but in a broader sense, it was one of the mathematical operations that real people rely on to more easily function in the real world.

Furthermore, by placing the addition in the context of a realistic situation (as opposed to a drill or practice sheet), it allows for the classroom examination of alternative solutions. For example, the problem could be solved using multiplication (*$4.36 × 3 = $13.08*). In the course of further conjecture and discussion, the problem could be used to extend students' mathematical problem-solving strategies if they considered the following: What if the headbands have gone on sale at half price? How about a "buy one, get one free sale"? If Chris has $15.00, would he have enough to buy the headbands? If so, how much will he have left after he buys them?

# Two-Step Problems

Two-step problems involve scenarios in which two calculations are needed in order to be able to arrive at the solution. Students follow the same problem-solving process as previously discussed—read, decide, estimate, work, explain—but multiple calculations will be completed before a solution is reached. The *Two-Step Problems* activity sheet (Figure 2.8) provides a framework for students to use while working these types of problems.

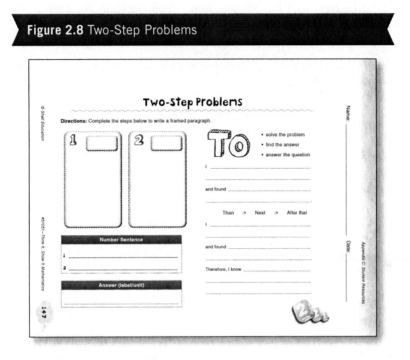

**Figure 2.8** Two-Step Problems

To use the *Two-Step Problems* activity sheet, students first write their labels or units in the rectangle at the top of the first work-area box. Then, they work their first problem in the work area on the far left and write their number sentences in the Number Sentences box on line one. They do the same thing with the second operation of the problem in the second work area and write their number sentences on line two of the Number Sentences box. They record their final answers with the labels or units in the Answer (label/unit) box. A number model version of the *One-Step Problems* and *Two-Step Problems* activity sheets can be found on the Digital Resource CD.

Students then use the framed paragraph to write about their solution. They start by choosing the phrase that they want to use in the first sentence of their paragraphs and follow with the words that explain the first mathematical operations they completed. They finish these sentences by writing the answers from their first number sentences in the space after *I*. They start their second sentences by choosing a transition/sequence word—*then*, *next*, *after that*—and following it with the explanation of their second operation. They write this answer after the words *and found*. They complete the paragraph with *Therefore, I know* and write the solution to the problem. As suggested with the *One-Step Problem* activity sheet, students' final or concluding sentences must directly answer the question that they underlined in the problem.

Below is an example of a two-step word problem.

Miranda and Joyce love to collect and trade seashells when they are at the beach together. One afternoon, Miranda had collected 31 shells when she and Joyce started trading. She traded 8 of her biggest shells for 15 of Joyce's small shells. How many shells did Miranda have then? Explain how you worked the problem.

Just as with one-step problems, students need practice reading, setting up, and solving these types of problems in order to be successful independently.

## 1. READ THE PROBLEM

- What is happening in the problem?
- What do I know?
- What don't I know
- What is the problem asking me to find out?

With step 1, students should mentally visualize the situation, explain it in their own words to a learning partner or in a small group, and/or draw a visual representation of what is happening in the problem. Also, the whole class would discuss whether the fact that Miranda traded her biggest shells for Joyce's small shells is important information when answering what the problem is asking them to figure out. As with the *One-Step Problems* activity sheet, students circle the number facts and underline the question of the problem.

As a result of careful reading and discussion, students should be able to answer the following questions:

- **What is happening in the problem?**
  Two girls, Miranda and Joyce, like to trade seashells when they are at the beach

- **What do I know?**
  Miranda collected 31 seashells.
  Miranda gave 8 of her shells to Joyce.
  Joyce gave Miranda 15 of her shells.

- **What don't I know?**
  I don't know how many seashells Miranda ended up with after they traded.

- **What is the problem asking me to find?**
  The problem is asking me to find out how many shells Miranda had at the end.

 **Decide**

- What operation(s) will I need to do to solve the problem?

- What problem-solving strategy should I use?

With step 2, students should identify the operations that are needed to solve the problem. When doing this type of problem for the first time, it is important to do this as a class in order for students to see that one calculation must be completed in order for the final solution to be correct. They need to understand that order matters. In this problem, the clue words *how many…have then* are not immediately helpful in determining the needed operations, so students need to comprehend the overall situation of the problem in order to solve it. The first operation and calculation that must be completed is subtracting 8 from 31—the shells that Miranda gave Joyce. The second operation and calculation is adding 15 to the number of shells that Miranda now has—the difference found in the first problem. Discussion could lead to another way to solve the problem—adding the difference between the traded shells and Miranda's total (15 − 8 = 7, 31 + 7 = 38 shells)—so be mindful to praise alternative solutions when problems can be solved multiple ways.

There are many problem-solving strategies that could be used to solve this problem, the most obvious being to draw a picture and to use an equation. Students should have the opportunity to choose a strategy that makes sense to them. However, feedback should be given in order to help students understand over time which strategies are most efficient for particular types of problems.

### 3. Make an Estimation

○ What is a reasonable answer?

In step 3, estimation is used to get a ballpark solution to the problem. This, again, is important so that students have a way to gauge how reasonable their final solutions are. Here is one student's process for using estimation with this problem:

Since 31 can be rounded to 30 and 8 rounded to 10, I can subtract 10 from 30 in my head, giving me 20. Then, I add the 3 fives in 15 by skip-counting from 20 by 5s… 20, 25, 30, 35. So my estimate is 35 shells.

### 4. Work the Problem

○ Check my work.

### 5. Explain My Math Thinking in Writing

Students complete the process by using the *Two-Step Problems* activity sheet to support them as they solve the problem and write about their mathematical thinking. On the next page is an example of a student-completed *Two-Step Problems* activity sheet and the final written paragraph (Figure 2.9).

**Figure 2.9** Sample Two-Step Problems

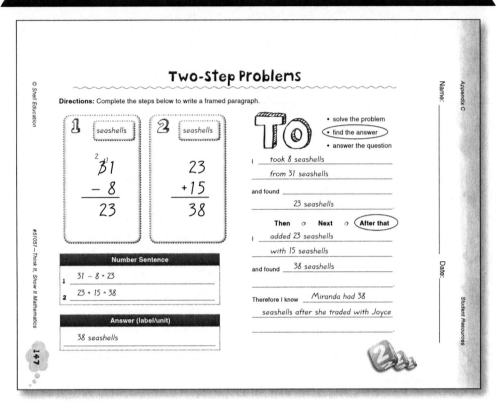

To find the answer, I took 8 seashells from 31 seashells and found 23 seashells. After that, I added 23 seashells with 15 seashells and found 38 seashells. Therefore, I know Miranda had 38 seashells after she traded with Joyce.

3rd Grade Student

# Final Thoughts on One- and Two-Step Procedural Writing

The *One-Step Problems* and *Two-Step Problems* activity sheets lay the groundwork for procedural writing in mathematics. They prompt and guide students to write clearly and precisely and to scaffold the use of the language and vocabulary of mathematics. By becoming familiar with its linguistic structure and terminology, students learn what mathematical writing "sounds" like. As they grow older and encounter more difficult problems and mathematical concepts, they'll be able to explain their problem-solving strategies with greater confidence. They are, after all, mathematically empowered students in the making.

Here are other students' examples of how Miranda and Joyce's seashell trading session might have been worked and explained. You will notice how these students expanded the language of the framed paragraph to include math vocabulary words such as *difference* and *sum* and also how some teachers want their students to spell out the number words.

> To answer the question, I subtracted the 8 seashells from 15 seashells and found a difference of 7 seashells. Next, I added 7 seashells plus 31 seashells and found a sum of 38 seashells. Therefore, I know that Miranda ended up with a total of 38 seashells to take home.
>
> 3rd Grade Student

> To solve the problem, I worked the problem of thirty-one seashells minus eight sea shells and found a difference of twenty-three. Next, I added the twenty-three seashells and fifteen seashells and found thirty-eight seashells. Therefore, I know that Miranda had a grand total of thirty-eight seashells.
>
> 3rd Grade Student

It may appear to some that these framed paragraphs produce a stilted, rather prescriptive-sounding text in contrast to the natural, more creative expression of students. It can be argued, however, that this is precisely what students are meant to do in the early stages of the learning process. If they internalize the basic language to use with a procedural explanation, then they can focus on the mathematics and simply fall back on what language to use.  It becomes very natural to them.  These framed paragraphs act as what I call a "mental template."  Furthermore, after students have gained a level of proficiency with these paragraphs, they can be encouraged to embellish them a bit, as is shown in the final example below.

> Michael and his friends were always counting things.  One day, they wanted to see how many DVDs they had between them.  They asked me to help.  So, first we counted how many each had.  Then to find the answer, I added Michael's 6 DVDs and Sid's 12 DVDs, and Sean's whopping 54 DVDs and found 72 DVDs. Therefore, we knew that Michael and friends had 72 DVDs altogether.
>
> 3rd Grade Student

# Rich, Complex Problems

As students continue down the path of mathematical learning, the expectation of the complexity of their mathematical understanding increases. They are expected to be able to solve problems in more than one way and explain their thought process more deeply or defend their solution. These types of problems are often multifaceted, mathematically challenging, and presented more as how they might be experienced in real life. They are often referred to as rich, complex problems.

During the summer, Henry earns $5.00 per hour babysitting and $4.00 per hour mowing lawns.

Part A: Henry babysat a total of 48 hours. How much money did he earn babysitting?

Part B: Including the 48 hours of babysitting, Henry earned a total of $308.00 by the end of the summer. How many hours did he spend mowing lawns?

(2004 CSAP Released Items Grade 5 Mathematics)

Here students are challenged with going beyond simply figuring out how much money Henry would make babysitting (48 hours times $5.00 equals $240.00). They also have to determine how many hours he mowed lawns by first subtracting the babysitting pay from the summer's total earnings ($308.00 minus $240.00 equals $68.00) and then dividing the $68.00 by $4.00 to conclude that Henry had mowed lawns for 17 hours—a three-step process involving multiplication, subtraction, and division and all with decimals. The window for possible errors is left wide open.

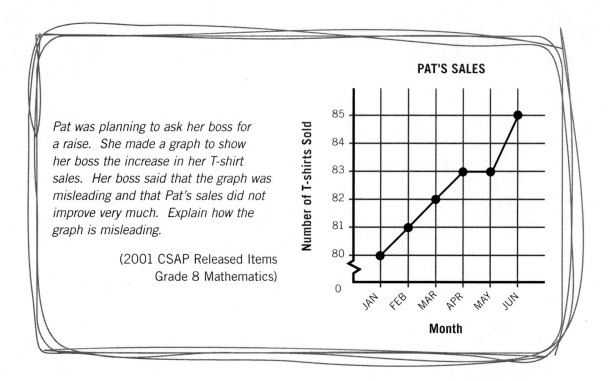

*Pat was planning to ask her boss for a raise. She made a graph to show her boss the increase in her T-shirt sales. Her boss said that the graph was misleading and that Pat's sales did not improve very much. Explain how the graph is misleading.*

(2001 CSAP Released Items
Grade 8 Mathematics)

Students first need to know how to read a line graph. Beyond that, they need to closely examine the data presented on the graph to figure out that, yes, Pat's sales had increased but not by very much, considering the fact that her sales numbers had started at 80 and over a period of six months had only increased by 5. Finally, students are expected to write an explanation justifying their conclusions.

Working with rich, complex problems like these, our students are forced to think and to persist even when the task is less obvious, and to use mathematics as a tool for interpreting information, solving problems, and finding solutions. Equally important in the process is their ability to articulate their mathematical reasoning coherently.

## Try It! ✏️

In an effort to connect mathematics to the real world, many teachers create and use problems that are derived from actual ongoing classroom and community experiences and extensions to other subject areas.

# Mathematical "Think-Alouds"

As students begin working with rich, complex problems, they should employ a step-by-step, analytically reasoned approach. But this type of methodical thinking rarely occurs naturally in students. They often fall back on the strategy I call "taking mathematical potshots at the problem." They say, "I'll add. No, that doesn't work. I'll divide. That doesn't work either. Maybe I should factor." What they are hoping is that they will magically stumble on the "right answer" and be done with it. The essential groundwork needed to help students develop into the type of mathematical thinkers we want them to become is having them learn and explore math in an environment where mathematical thinking is made visible and having a learning community where on a regular basis students hear the teacher's or other students' thinking processes while solving a problem. This approach is most often referred to as a "think-aloud," and it is where teachers verbalize for their students what they are thinking as they work through a problem. Frank Smith, an educational writer on thinking and learning, contends in his book, *Writing and the Writer* that "human beings learn through 'demonstration.' Demonstrations not only of what can be done and how it can be done, but what the person doing it feels about the act" (1982, 32). Mathematical reasoning is learned in the classroom through the regular demonstrations of its use. Valuable questions to verbalize a response to as you describe your thinking process are as follows:

- How did you know?

- Why do you think your solution makes sense?

- What steps did you use to figure that out?

- Is there another way of solving that problem?

- Can you prove that your solution is correct?

Another possibility is to actively involve the whole class in what I call a "group think-aloud."

> *Who can tell me what we will know if we do this operation? Is there another approach that we might use? From our estimation, does this figure seem reasonable? If we do this, what will it tell us, and is that what we are looking for? Could someone draw a flow chart for the steps that we have identified so far?*

# Process Maps

Another classroom activity that teachers can use to support this type of thinking is called a *process map*, in which students record the step-by-step process they use in solving a problem. Here, students take a problem and, working individually or in small groups, craft a creative "map" for how they solved the problem. It can be a narrative map using words to map out the process or an illustrated map using pictures and symbols. Some students even like to create a PowerPoint® presentation complete with sounds and images or other creative approaches. Here, as an example, is a "process map" using the idea of a recipe that a group of fifth-grade students created.

Between Matt's parents and his grandparents, Matt got a big check for his allowance. He saved one-half of the money and spent the rest. He bought a sports magazine for $3.95, a used CD for $8.30, and a large Coke for $2.75. How much allowance did Matt receive?

**Process Map Steps**

1. Place the problem on a cutting board.

2. Examine it carefully. Determine what parts are needed for the final dish *(Matt saved one-half of his allowance, and he spent $3.95 on a sports magazine, $8.30 on a used CD, and $2.75 on a soda.)*

3. Using a sharp knife, slice this data from the problem and place each piece in a medium-size bowl.

4. Take only the pieces $3.95, $8.30, and $2.75 from the bowl and put them in the addition-operation pot. Add the necessary ingredients of addition facts, lined-up decimals, and regrouping. Boil until a sum is found.

5. Take the sum from the addition-operation pot and place it in the division operation pot.

6. Take the fraction $\frac{1}{2}$ and knead it until it converts to a 2. Blend and stir the 2 with the sum in the division pot until the quotient is firm.

7. Place the quotient in a small dish. Label and serve with a smile.

# Solving Rich, Complex Problems

When solving a rich, complex problem, students should use the same step-by-step thinking approach explained in Chapter 2—Read, Decide, Estimate, Work, and Explain. The *Explain and Gain the Concept* activity sheet supports these systematic steps and provides students with the opportunity to analyze a given problem and then explain their mathematical thinking.

**Figure 3.1** Explain and Gain the Concept

**Step 1:** This first step has students address and state the "givens" of a problem:

- What is happening in the problem?
- What do I know?
- What is my data?

Students then record their data in the box labeled *Data: Number Facts.* Then they consider the following.

- What don't I know?
- What is the problem asking me to find out?

They continue by stating, using a complete sentence, exactly what their answer will tell them when they have finished the problem in the box labeled *What Will My Answer Tell Me?* This is an important step in the process because after they have written their narrative at the bottom half of the sheet, they can underline and draw a line from the concluding sentence of their paragraph up to the statement in this box to see if, in fact, they have answered it.

**Step 2:** Students use their data to write the number sentence(s) of the operation(s) they need to do to solve the problem.

**Step 3:** Students use estimation to decide upon a reasonable solution to the problem.

**Step 4:** Students use the actual workspace and complete their calculation(s).

Consider the following problem:

Chen's family is planning a trip to Santa Fe for the weekend. His dad asked Chen to use the map and determine how many miles it will take them to drive there and back. After looking at the map, Chen told him that a round trip would be a total of 621 miles. "Good," said his dad. "Now, since we know our car gets, on the average, 23 miles per gallon, and gas, at the moment, is priced at $3.96 a gallon, how much money will we need to budget to get to Santa Fe and back on our trip?" Explain how Chen can find an accurate answer for his dad.

The top half of the student activity sheet might look like what we see in Figure 3.2.

**Figure 3.2** Explain and Gain the Concept Student Sample

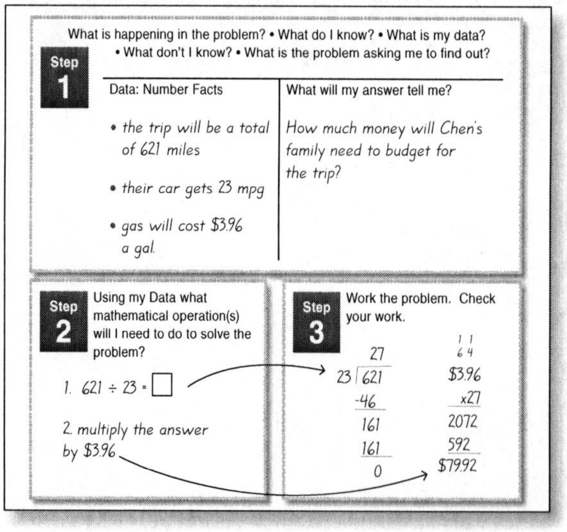

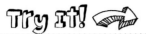

Have students draw lines from each of their operations in Step 2 to where they completed the computations in the box for Step 3. This reminds them to check and see if they did each of the operations.

**Step 5:** With the first three steps completed, students are now ready to write their narratives.

Before students can truly be successful writing longer math narratives that are required by the nature of more rich, complex problems, they need to become fluent with the language of mathematics. Mathematics has its own language that is distinctly different from the way we talk and communicate in everyday life. Nobody talks—at least I don't think anybody does—like this around the dinner table:

*"Since I know that our trip to Santa Fe and back will be a total of 621 miles and that our car gets on average 23 miles per gallon, I will need to first divide the 621 miles by 23 mpg. I will find that we need 27 gallons for the trip. Then, I will need to multiply the 27 times $3.96 because the cost of gas is $3.96 per gallon. Doing this, I find an answer of $106.92. Therefore, I know that we will need to budget $106.92 for the gas portion of our trip to Santa Fe."*

*"Pass the dressing, please."*

In math, however, students need to think and write with just such formulaic clarity and algorithmic precision. In doing so, they will be using their math vocabulary in correct mathematical sentences. The trouble many students run into, of course, is incorrectly writing sentences with operations that do not have the commutative (or order) property. They write *I divided 621 into 23* or *I subtracted $1.55 from the $0.59.* One of the ways to help students learn to write sentences that are algebraically correct is to provide a bulletin board of expanded full sentences using the correct mathematical vocabulary.

Here are some examples of displayed written responses from completed problems with their specific math vocabulary underlined.

---

I needed to <u>add</u> the 25 students from Mr. Smith's class <u>plus</u> the 17 students from Mrs. Kilgore's class. I <u>found a total</u> of 42 students.

I <u>subtracted</u> the $0.59 from the $1.55 that Mike had and <u>found</u> $0.76. With the $0.76, Mike would just barely have enough money <u>left</u> to buy the $0.75 bag of popcorn.

I decided to <u>divide</u> the 82 chairs <u>by</u> the 9 rows and <u>found an answer</u> of 9 with a <u>remainder</u> of 1. Therefore, we could have 9 rows of chairs with 9 chairs in each row and have only 1 chair <u>left over</u>.

---

An extension of this is to have students team up with each other and see how many different sentences they can write for each of the operations. As a quick example, *I divided the 82 chairs by the nine rows* could also be written as follows:

- I divided 9 rows into the 82 chairs
- I thought to myself, 9 times what is about 82?
- I added 9 plus 9 plus 9 plus 9 until I reached 81.

Figure 3.3 shows a poster that can be displayed at math learning centers or at the other locations in the classroom for reference. It outlines the essential elements, or "ground rules," for writing a math narrative. It may also be helpful for students to have smaller copies of it in their individual math journals. The guidelines are as follows:

- Use math vocabulary in correct math sentences
- Include all your data (number facts)
- Use transition words
- Explain the why of your steps

- Write in complete sentences
- Label your answer
- Proofread your writing

**Figure 3.3** Explaining Your Math Thinking in Writing

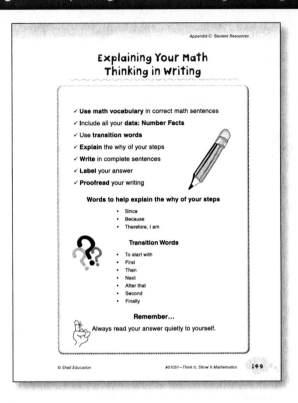

Let's examine each of the elements individually.

## Use Mathematical Vocabulary Correctly

In mathematical writing we are, of course, using the domain (mathematics-specific) vocabulary of mathematics—the words needed to accurately and clearly communicate mathematical concepts and processes. Examples of these types of words include *addition, subtraction, decimal point, common denominator, equivalent, mixed number, height, length, median,* and *mean.*

In learning to use this specialized vocabulary correctly, students first need to recognize math vocabulary in print. From there, we can see an overlapping progression of skills and understanding in order to be able to fully grasp a word's usage in the language of mathematics.

Word recognition
    Its meaning
        Its relationship to a concept
            Its correct usage in the language of mathematics

## Strategies for Learning Mathematical Vocabulary

### Math Word Walls

Many teachers have key math vocabulary words displayed on bulletin boards (most often called "Word Walls"), where the words are reviewed regularly until students can recognize and read the vocabulary they are using at their grade level. The words and their meanings can also get logged in student math journals.

Utilize word walls in the following ways:

1. Highlight words with bright colors.

2. Vary the word organization (alphabetically, grouped by concept, matched with meanings).

3. Include abbreviations and mathematical symbols.

4. Develop games and activities to use with the words that encourage students to interact with the words.

From the recognition of words and their meanings, students need to more fully understand the words by connecting them to a mathematical concept or process. For example, students need to see that the words *subtract, take away, minus,* and *difference* are all descriptors used with the operation of subtraction. Similarly, students need to group words such as *meter, milliliter, gram,* and *centimeter* as metric measurements. There are a variety of activities to help students in this area.

### Concept Groups

Students (individually or in a collaborative team) take a list of math vocabulary words and sort them into concept groups. They then justify or explain why and how they grouped the words. They may choose to use a Venn diagram or a triple Venn diagram to identify how some words belong in more than one concept group.

## Concept Webbing and Brainstorming

The teacher writes individual math words on small pieces of paper and places them in a bowl. Students each pull out one word and start constructing a web by thinking of all the words and ideas mathematically connected to that word. When they have come up with all that they can think of, they pair up with other students to continue brainstorming. Many times, this activity can be extended into having students work together to create categories with their own original (and creative) labels for mathematically related words and ideas. Students are then asked to justify and explain the reasoning behind their labels.

## Mathematical Snapper-Clappers

A graduate student of mine created a poetic form of reinforcing vocabulary concepts. In this strategy, she used math content and applied a simple rhythmic and rhyming pattern with corresponding kinesthetic hand motions frequently used in writing poetry in language arts instruction. To represent the first beat in the pattern, you slap both legs with your hands (This is shown by the number 1). To represent the second beat in the pattern, you clap both hands (This is shown by the number 2). You snap your fingers to represent the third beat in the poem (This is shown by the number 3). Below is the pattern shown in conjunction with a model poem.

**Old man crow**
 1  2   3
*Slap clap snap*


**He did sew**
 1  2   3
*Slap clap snap*


**On his chest a crooked bow.**
 1  2,  1   2,   1  2   3
*Slap clap, slap clap, slap clap snap*

Here are some student samples written about multiplication. Notice that the rhyming and syllabic pattern is the same as the sample shown above, but the numbers and motion cues are not included.

I'll tell you
Forty-two
Six times seven in a long canoe.


Seven times two
What to do
Fourteen feet but only one shoe.


Don't be late
Forty-eight
Twelve times four could be your date.

## Concept File Cards

With this strategy, students use six 3 × 5 index cards to record information about a mathematical concept and record details that help them understand and apply the concept. Figure 3.4 outlines the details that should be recorded on each of the six cards. These cards are held together with a small binding ring or string and are referenced as needed. A set could also be left in the math learning center so that they may be referenced by anyone in the class.

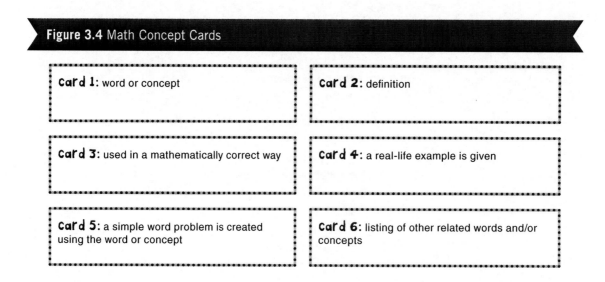

**Figure 3.4** Math Concept Cards

**Card 1**: word or concept

**Card 2**: definition

**Card 3**: used in a mathematically correct way

**Card 4**: a real-life example is given

**Card 5**: a simple word problem is created using the word or concept

**Card 6**: listing of other related words and/or concepts

Below is an example using the concept of fractions.

| | |
|---|---|
| **Card 1**: fractions | **Card 2**: a ratio of numbers or variables |
| **Card 3**: $\frac{3}{4}$ x 100 = 75 | **Card 4**: One-half of our semester grade will be from completed homework. The other half will be from tests and quizzes. |
| **Card 5**: William's football team only lost one-fifth of its games this season. If the season was a total of 15 games, how many did William's team win? | **Card 6**: ratio, variables, simplified, rational expression, denominator, numerator, common denominator, compound fraction, improper fraction, proper fraction, mixed numbers, integer |

## Include All Your Data (Number Facts)

The next ground rule for a math narrative is that in their written explanations, students must include and bring together all of their data. As discussed, part of our analysis of a problem is the determination of its critical information—what we have referred to as number facts. In the case of Chen's planned trip to Santa Fe, the number facts are:

- The trip to Santa Fe and back is 621 miles.
- Their car gets 23 miles per gallon.
- Gas is priced at $3.96 a gallon.

A written explanation would then need to incorporate each of these number facts (that is the reason we recorded them in the Step 1 box) even if the operations include mathematics that students feel they could do in their heads. This is important in order to truly understand the process that students go through in order to find a solution for this problem. For example, let's take a look at this problem.

> John went to the mall with some friends. He spent $11.84 on a new CD. Then, he spent one-fourth of that amount on a sports magazine. In addition, when he and his friends got hungry, he bought a slice of pizza for $1.50 and a soda for half of the price of the pizza. How much did he spend altogether while he was at the mall? Explain how you found your answer.

The number facts are that John spent:

- $11.84 on a new CD

- one-fourth of $11.84 for a sports magazine

- $1.50 for a slice of pizza

- one–half of $1.50 on a soda

Most students can easily do one-half of $1.50 in their heads, but if in their written explanation the figure $0.75 suddenly appears out of nowhere, the clarity of the response is weakened.  Students need to understand that they certainly can do some of the operations in their heads, but they simply need to inform the reader what they are doing.  It can be written like this: *Since I knew that one-half of $1.50 was $0.75, I added that to the other items.*

## Use Transition/Sequence Words

When students are explaining how to solve a mathematical problem, they are producing a procedural text, and procedural texts need to follow a logical and readable sequence. As an illustration, if writing about how to care for a dog, there are many things that can be included in the the text: feeding it, taking it to the vet regularly, grooming it, giving it exercise.  The sequence, however, in which each of these activities is described is not critical to an overall understanding of the given topic.  This would be an example of an explanatory text.  On the other hand, if I try to explain how to download music from the Internet, the sequence of the steps described in the process is essential if the reader hopes to be able to follow and understand it.  This is where we have students use transition words, or as they are often called in math and science, "sequence" or "order" words. Effective use of these helps them produce a procedural text that is both readable and logical. These transition words include:

- *first*
- *then*
- *next*

- *after that*
- *second*
- *finally*

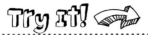

**Try It!**

When students finish the drafts of their paragraphs, have them circle their transition words to see how these helped them sequence their text logically.

## Explain the Why of All Your Steps

What makes procedural writing ultimately logical and readable is exactly what makes the process of producing it so valuable. Students have to slow down and take it step by reasoned step. They can't skip steps, and each step has to be justified. In other words, students are forced to think methodically.

The activity sheet shown in Figure 3.5 can be used to support students as they record the procedural steps they follow and justify each step through a written explanation. Although very similar to the previous activity sheet, this activity sheet gives students additional support in justifying their procedures in order to be able to more clearly record procedural text in a more open-ended way (Figure 3.1). For additional support and suggestions on writing explanatory/procedural text, see Chapter 4.

**Figure 3.5** Thinking and Justifying Activity Sheet

Appendix C: Student Resources

Name: _____ Date: _____

### Thinking and Justifying

**Directions:** Complete the graphic organizer to explain your problem-solving process.

**Step 1** What is happening in the problem? • What do I know? • What is my data? • What don't I know? • What is the problem asking me to find out?

| Data: Number Facts | What will my answer tell me? |

Tell what steps you will need to do to solve the problem. **Step 2** Tell why you need to do these steps to solve the problem.

**Transition Words:** • to start with • then • next • after that • first • second • third • finally

**Why Words:** • since • because • therefore, I know

© Shell Education  #51051—Think It, Show It Mathematics  153

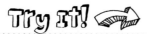

Using the *Thinking and Justifying* activity sheet (Figure 3.5), have students work collaboratively with a problem of the day.

## The Final Steps

The final steps of the process (with the exception of number 6) are the same requirements as for all writing tasks:

**5.** Write in complete sentences.

**6.** Label your answer.

**7.** Proofread your writing.

Students should be familiar with these types of tasks based on writing they do during language arts instruction.

## Student Responses to Rich, Complex Problems

Below and on the next few pages are some examples of other students' explanations of the rich, complex problem involving John at the mall presented previously. Please realize that these are not selected as examples of the best students' work but rather illustrations of typical types of responses that students make as they are learning to master the math narrative.

> Since John spent \$11.84 on a CD, I had to take $\frac{1}{4}$ of that amount to find how much he spent on a sports magazine. I divided \$11.84 by 4 and found \$2.96. Next, he spent \$1.50 on a slice of pizza, and I used $\frac{1}{2}$ of \$1.50 to see how much he spent on a drink. Because I knew half of \$1.50 is \$0.75, I had to add all of the prices to find how much he spent in all. Therefore, I know that John spent \$17.05 at the mall.
>
> 5th Grade Student

Since (*why statement*) John spent $11.84 on a new CD and one-fourth of that amount on a sports magazine (*what statement*), I first (*transition word*) divided $11.84 by 4 (*what statement*). I found $2.96 (*not allowed to write "I got"*). I then (*second transition word*) divided the $1.50 that John spent on the pizza in half (*what statement*) because (*why word*) he spent half of that amount on a drink (*why statement*). I did this in my head because I knew that half of $1.50 was $0.75 (*letting the reader know exactly where the $0.75 came from*). Finally (*another transition word*), I added up all four items (*what statement*) to find out what he had spent altogether at the mall (*why statement*) and found (*not allowed to write "I got"*) a total of $17.05. Therefore, I know (*to sound good and smart AND have the perfect concluding sentence*) that John spent a total of $17.05 when he went to the mall.

5th Grade Student

To start with, I had to divide 4 into $11.84 because John spent $\frac{1}{4}$ of $11.84 on a sports magazine. I found $2.96. Then, I divided $1.50 in half because John spent $\frac{1}{2}$ of $1.50 on a drink. This equaled $0.75. Finally, I added all of my answers together plus $11.84 and $1.50 because he also bought a CD and a slice of pizza. Therefore, I know that John spent a total of $17.05.

6th Grade Student

To start with, I divided $11.84 by 4 because the sports magazine was $\frac{1}{4}$ the cost of the CD ($11.84). I found out when I divided that I got $2.96 as an answer. So I concluded that the sports magazine was $2.96. I knew that $\frac{1}{2}$ of 1.50 was $0.75. So the drink cost $0.75. I added $2.96, $11.84, $0.75, and $1.50 together, and I found that he spent $17.05. Therefore, I know John spent $17.05 when he went to the mall.

6th Grade Student

When I went through this problem, I took three steps. First, since John bought a magazine for $\frac{1}{4}$ the cost of the CD, which was $11.84, I divided $11.84 by 4. I found an answer of $2.96. Then, I knew $\frac{1}{2}$ of $1.50 was $0.75, so I divided $1.50 by 2 just to be positive because John bought a pizza for $1.50 and a drink for half the price. Finally, I added $11.84 and $2.96 to $1.50 and .$0.75. I found $17.05. Therefore, I know what John spent on the 4 items when he was at the mall.

6th Grade Student

## Using Rubrics for Problem Solving

Rubrics can be a powerful tool to help students master certain skills. There are three reasons for this. First, using a well-designed rubric and introducing it to students before they begin a task removes the guesswork from what is expected of them. They have a concrete depiction of what makes a successful end product. In the case of a written response in math, they can reference the rubric's criteria for reaching proficiency. Second, a rubric gives a precise tool for providing targeted feedback to students. By using the specific criteria on the rubric as a guide, teachers can do more than simply give students grades or scores; teachers can show them exactly where they were off base as well as where they were right on the mark. A rubric is only as good as the support and feedback it generates for the learner. Finally, when students use the rubric in the scoring of each other's written responses, they practice how to evaluate their own.

**Figure 3.6** Explaining Your Math Thinking in Words

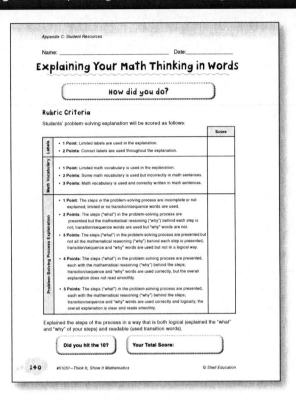

Figure 3.6 is a 10-point rubric that is used with the math narrative. Let's take a look at its criteria.

## Rubric Criteria

Students' problem-solving explanation will be scored as follows:

## Labels

- **1 Point**: Limited labels are used in the explanation.

- **2 Points**: Correct labels are used throughout the explanation.

Here, it's stressed that the answers must include labels. Labels are the bedrock of statements in a math narrative. Many times, students (most likely as a result of earlier training) regularly and conscientiously place a label in their concluding sentences. For example, in a problem where students were determining how many slices of pizza each of four friends would get at a party, they would say:

*Therefore, everyone at Jean's party will get four pieces of <u>pizza</u>.*

However, before that final sentence they might have written:

*I multiplied 2 times 8* instead of *I multiplied the 2 <u>pizzas</u> times the 8 <u>slices</u> they were cut into.*

By allowing a possible two points for this criteria, the paper can be awarded one point for a label given in the final sentence and go on to show the student exactly what was needed to get the full two points. Remind students that using labels and details throughout your response connects the reader to the situation of the original problem.

## Math Vocabulary

- **1 Point**: Limited math vocabulary is used in the explanation.
- **2 Points**: Some math vocabulary is used but incorrectly in math sentences.
- **3 Points**: Math vocabulary is used and correctly written in math sentences.

These criteria, as was emphasized earlier, get students to use the language of mathematics appropriately—the correct math terminology within a correct mathematical sentence. With its three-point spread, a student who writes *I divided the 16 slices into the 4 friends that would be eating and found that each would get 4 slices of pizza* can receive credit for having the math vocabulary (*divided*), but not the full three points because of the incorrectly written math sentence (*divided 16 into 4*)

## Problem-Solving Process Explanation

- **1 Point**: The steps in the problem-solving process are incomplete or not explained; limited or no transition/sequence words are used.
- **2 Points**: The steps ("what") in the problem-solving process are presented, but the mathematical reasoning ("why") behind the steps is not; transition/sequence words are used but "why" words are not.
- **3 Points**: The steps ("what") in the problem-solving process are presented but not all the mathematical reasoning ("why") behind each step is presented; transition/sequence and "why" words are used but not in a logical way.
- **4 Points**: The steps ("what") in the problem-solving process are presented, each with the mathematical reasoning ("why") behind the steps; transition/sequence and "why" words are used correctly, but the overall explanation does not read smoothly.
- **5 Points**: The steps ("what") in the problem-solving process are presented, each with mathematical reasoning ("why") behind each step; transition/sequence and "why" words are used correctly and logically; and the overall explanation is clear and reads smoothly.

This is the big-money winner of the rubric. Here, students have to put it all together and use all of the elements of math narrative in their text: *what* and *why* statements, *why* words, data, and labels, and an effective use of transition words. They are challenged by the rubric to **GO for a 10!**

## Learning by Scoring

As valuable as teachers' specific feedback is to students, equally beneficial is students evaluating their own and one another's responses. Figure 3.7 is a rubric that can be used to accomplish this. Arranged in small groups of three or four, students are given a problem and five written responses. They first analyze the problem in the work area in the top half of the sheet. When they agree on an answer, they then evaluate the first student's response according to the rubric's three criteria by putting a number in each of the boxes and calculating a total. They do the same with the remaining four responses.

**Figure 3.7** How Did They Do? Peer Scoring Rubric

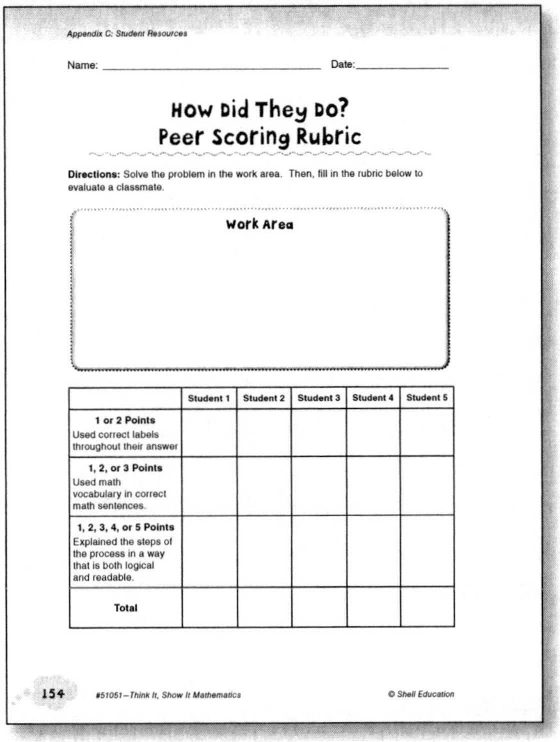

*Appendix C: Student Resources*

Name: ______________________ Date: __________

**How Did They Do?**
**Peer Scoring Rubric**

**Directions:** Solve the problem in the work area. Then, fill in the rubric below to evaluate a classmate.

**Work Area**

| | Student 1 | Student 2 | Student 3 | Student 4 | Student 5 |
|---|---|---|---|---|---|
| **1 or 2 Points** Used correct labels throughout their answer | | | | | |
| **1, 2, or 3 Points** Used math vocabulary in correct math sentences. | | | | | |
| **1, 2, 3, 4, or 5 Points** Explained the steps of the process in a way that is both logical and readable. | | | | | |
| **Total** | | | | | |

154 #51051—Think It, Show It Mathematics © Shell Education

Using the problem below, let's see how a group of third graders scored five different responses. You may want to use the rubric and see how you would have scored each response *before* reading on to see the third graders' scores.

Mrs. Forever Peeling is having a big Thanksgiving dinner. She bought three 10 pound bags of potatoes. In each bag, there were 24 potatoes. She peeled half of the potatoes for the big meal. How many potatoes did she peel altogether? Explain how you found your answer.

## Student 1 Sample

- - - - - - - - - - - - - - - - - - - - - - - - - - - - - - - - - - -

First, I took the bags and multiplied it by 24. Then, I found 72. Next, I took 72 and divided by 2 and found 36. Therefore, I know Mrs. Forever Peeling peeled 36.

## Student 2 Sample

- - - - - - - - - - - - - - - - - - - - - - - - - - - - - - - - - - -

First, I added 24 potatoes and 2 more 24 potatoes, and I found 72 potatoes. Then, I divided 72 potatoes by 2. Finally, I found 36 potatoes.

## Student 3 Sample

- - - - - - - - - - - - - - - - - - - - - - - - - - - - - - - - - - -

First, I took the 3 bags and multiplied it by 24 because she had 3 bags and each bag had 24 potatoes. Then, I found 72. Next, I took 72 and divided it by 2 and found 36. Therefore, I know Mrs. Forever Peeling peeled 36 potatoes.

## Student 4 Sample

- - - - - - - - - - - - - - - - - - - - - - - - - - - - - - - - - - -

Since Mrs. Forever Peeling bought 3 ten-pound bags of potatoes with 24 potatoes in each bag, I had to multiply 24 potatoes by the 3 bags, giving me a total of 72 potatoes. I then divided the 72 potatoes by 2 because she had only peeled half of them for her Thanksgiving dinner and $72 \div 2 = 36$. Therefore, I know Mrs. Forever Peeling had peeled 36 potatoes.

## Student 5 Sample

- - - - - - - - - - - - - - - - - - - - - - - - - - - - - - - - - - -

First, I divided 24 potatoes by 2 because the problem said that she only peeled half of the potatoes. This told me that half of each bag of potatoes would equal 12 potatoes. Since there were 3 ten pound bags, I multiplied 3 times 12 and found 36. Therefore, I know that Mrs. Forever Peeling peeled 36 potatoes.

So how did your scores compare with the ones students came up with? See Figure 3.8.

**Figure 3.8** How Did They Do? Student Scores

*Appendix C* *Student Resources*

Name: ______________________________ Date: ______________

## How Did They Do? Peer Scoring Rubric

**Directions:** Solve the problem in the work area. Then, fill in the rubric below to evaluate a classmate.

**Work Area**

| | Student 1 | Student 2 | Student 3 | Student 4 | Student 5 |
|---|---|---|---|---|---|
| **1 or 2 Points** Used correct labels throughout their answer | 0 | 1 | 2 | 2 | 2 |
| **1, 2, or 3 Points** Used math vocabulary in correct math sentences. | 3 | 1 | 3 | 3 | 3 |
| **1, 2, 3, 4, or 5 Points** Explained the steps of the process in a way that is both logical and readable. | 2 | 2 | 4 | 5 | 5 |
| **Total** | 5 | 4 | 9 | 10 | 10 |

154 *#51051—Think It, Show It Mathematics* © Shell Education

Having observed this process many times in different classrooms, I believe that agreeing on the score is least important. Instead, it is the dialogue generated between students—their talking, explaining, and listening—that results in the biggest learning opportunities. I have eavesdropped on the groups and heard them hashing out the scores as carefully and analytically as any group of teachers with whom I've led through the same procedure. What students are really doing during this process is verbally rehearsing good thinking—the same good thinking that I want them to apply with their own written responses.

## Using Student Samples as Exemplars

Looking at the answers of Students 4 and 5, I am sure you would agree that even though they had approached and solved the problem with different strategies, they were both still able to score a well-deserved 10.

If you look closely at the work of Student 4, however, you see that while it has successfully applied all the elements of a math narrative (*what* and *why* statements, *why* words, transition/sequence words, labels, and data) to easily earn a 10, it has been done with exceptional clarity. The clarity comes from how it aligned with the context of the problem. The first sentence of the answer sets the stage for the situation presented in the problem. A specific woman bought a specific number of bags of potatoes with a specific number of potatoes in each.

*Since Mrs. Forever Peeling bought 3 ten pound bags of potatoes with 24 potatoes in each bag…*

The reader knows right off the bat some of the contextual details of the problem because the mathematical operation and reason *why* are anchored with those details. Compare that with the first sentence of Student 1.

*First I took the bags and multiplied it by 24.*

Here the reader knows little or nothing. How many bags? Bags of what?

Later in the paragraph, Student 4 explains the "why" as well as the occasion for her mathematical operation.

*I then divided the 72 potatoes by 2 because she had only peeled half of them for her Thanksgiving dinner…*

Examples of work as demonstrated by Student 4, what I call "exemplary papers," should be saved to share with other classes.

## Try It! 

Take an exemplary paper from a problem that your class has not solved yet and display it for all students to see. Have the students—who are not familiar with the problem—write in their journals what they think the original problem was. Then present another response like that of Student 1 to show them the difference.

Appendix E contains other sample problems and exemplary student responses.

# Writing to Further Learning

## The Writing Process in Math

Math curriculum presents endless and creative avenues for students' writing. Along with growth and further learning about math concepts and topics as a result of their extended reading and research, students can integrate math writing with the writing process as it is implemented in their language arts classes. Below are some ideas for suggested types of writing that can be incorporated into the math classroom.

- reports
- instructions
- journal entries
- manuals

- reaction papers
- applications
- arguments
- position papers

- personal narratives
- fictional stories
- biographies
- letters

Writing in math is best facilitated proceeding in exactly the same routines as applied in Writer's Workshop where the writing process is used. This process is stressed in the *Common Core State Standard's Production and Distribution of writing*: "develop and strengthen writing as needed by planning, revising, editing, rewriting, or trying a new approach" (2010, 1). Here are the stages common to most writing workshops:

1. Prewriting/Planning

2. Rough or First Draft

3. Revision

4. Editing

5. Final Draft/Proofreading

6. Sharing and/or Publishing

It is important to know that although the writing process appears to proceed in a linear, step-by-step sequence, the process is much more recursive by nature. During the process, students often need to revert or swing back to activities characteristic of an earlier stage. A student may discover that while he is working on his first draft, he needs an explanation of something he is unsure of and must return to the prewriting and research stage, or while revising, realize that new information needs to be included in the piece, resulting in his having to return to the planning stage.

## Prewriting/Planning

**To select a topic, assemble and begin to organize content, identify the writing purpose and type of writing, and generate vocabulary.**

Prewriting/planning in math allows students time to get their ideas on paper and gauge their own background on the topic they are writing about. It can also help them figure out how much research they need to do in order to be successful. There is a range of prewriting/planning strategies that teachers can introduce their students to, for example:

- webs
- word clusters
- free writes
- brainstorms
- outlines
- maps

- word mines
- graphic organizers
- lists
- data charts
- Venn diagrams
- T-charts

The *Thinking through Your Writing* prewriting activity sheet (Figure 4.1) supports students as they plan their writing on a specific topic. Here, students identify a topic and the purpose for writing. Often the type of writing (e.g., explanatory, first-person narrative) is identified as well. The "Information Questions" section allows students to plan questions that might be best researched for the assignment. Finally, students record the form in which their writing should be submitted (e.g., paragraphs, poem, list).

**Figure 4.1** Thinking through Your Writing

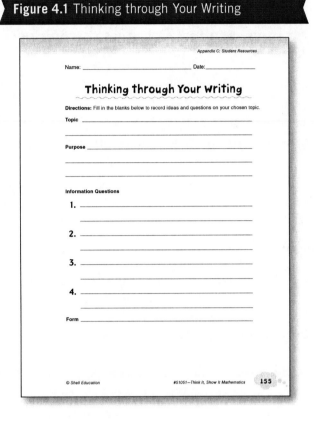

*Appendix C: Student Resources*

Name: _____ Date: _____

## Thinking through Your Writing

**Directions:** Fill in the blanks below to record ideas and questions on your chosen topic.

Topic _____

_____

Purpose _____

_____

_____

**Information Questions**

1. _____

_____

2. _____

_____

3. _____

_____

4. _____

_____

Form _____

© Shell Education          #51051—Think It, Show It Mathematics          **155**

## Rough Draft or First Draft

**Write using ideas generated as part of the prewriting phase and based on research, data, or other methods of acquiring information.**

In order for students to be able to begin writing, they must conduct research or gather information to support the ideas they came up with during the prewriting phase. This can be done by going to the library and reading books, exploring the Internet for information, talking with experts in the field, or other methods. Students should be encouraged to write their ideas in an organized way, all the while knowing that there will be other opportunities to fine-tune their work. Although spelling, punctuation, and grammar are always important, they will be addressed later in the writing process, so they should not become stumbling blocks for students at this stage.

## Revision

**Look again, to reexamine and make changes that improve the content, organization, and clarity of the writing.**

In math, the revision process allows students to review the content they have included in their writing and consider what might need clarification, what needs to be added or shifted around, and what might need to be deleted. A common acronym, ARMS can be used to help students remember the content revision process:

- Add content

- Remove content

- Move content

- Substitute for different word, idea, or content

Students know that at the revision stage, they are "re-seeing" or reconsidering their drafts. Sometimes, students do this individually, or other times, they work in pairs or groups, commenting on one another's drafts. During this stage, students are not only considering the organization of the piece (*Does it follow a logical progression?*) and its clarity (*Is it easy to read, follow, and understand?*) but also taking a critical look at the actual content (*Is the content accurate, complete, and contain no misconceptions?*). Other stylistic considerations during the revision process are: *Does it engage the reader? Is its vocabulary used effectively?*

Many times during the revision stage, I may want to have individual writing conferences with students during which we discuss their papers probing with questions like these:

- What do you think of your work so far? Are there any problems?

- Is there anything else you think you might need to say about your topic? Do you think you need more information?

- Have you included enough detail? Have you elaborated enough?

- Is there another way to look at this idea or another way to explain it?

- What did you mean to say here? Can it be made clearer for the reader?

- Tell how this idea is connected to the other ideas in the piece.

- Here, you are almost repeating word-for-word what you said earlier. How might you revise that?

- Are there any facts that you think you might need to double-check?

## Editing

**Identify and correct mistakes in grammar, punctuation, spelling, and capitalization.**

The editing phase is a time for students to specifically review their work to look for mistakes in grammar, punctuation, spelling, and capitalization. The acronym CUPS can be used to remind students of what they should be looking for:

- **C**apitalization

- **U**sage

- **P**unctuation

- **S**pelling

At this stage of the writing process, students know that they are to mark up their rough drafts using standard editing marks that indicate where they need to make corrections on their final drafts—mistakes with mechanics and the conventions of capitalization, usage, punctuation, and spelling. The language used for this is *Notice and Consider* and *Think Through and Decide*. Students are to read their draft "noticing and considering" possible errors. Along with the many other writing issues, we always need to focus on the typical—and maddening—homophone errors that students notoriously make. These are called *high glare errors* because they are the types of errors we find glaring on our pages.

- *whose* versus *who's*

- *your* versus *you're*

- *to, two,* and *too*

- *their, there,* and *they're*

- *our* versus *are*

As any teacher knows, this list certainly could continue. Secondly, students have a record of their "personal error patterns" in their writer's notebooks. These are the types of errors with which they individually have frequent problems, such as run-on sentences and fragments. While they are going through their drafts "noticing and considering," they are to "think through." *Do I need an apostrophe here? Is that the correct use of* sense? They then, of course, have to "decide." *This needs to be corrected here. I definitely will need to capitalize this.* It is also important for the classroom to contain many reference books and aids for them to use during this process. Having marked-up their papers with their editing marks, they are now ready to rewrite or word process their final copies. Figure 4.2 is a diagram of the editing process as I teach it to my students.

**Figure 4.2** The Editing Process

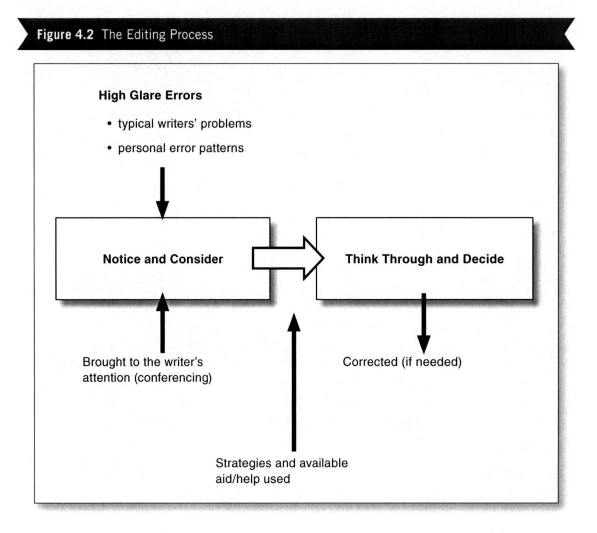

## Final Draft and Proofreading

**Find and correct errors and oversights as the final copy is completed either by being word processed or written by hand.**

Here, students write out their final copies, amending the text with the revisions they have decided on and making the corrections that are needed from their editing decisions. However, before they turn the paper in, they are to proofread it one last time. Again, they are to double-check their mechanics and conventions and also look for any oversights that might have occurred during the rewriting. Had they inadvertently left something out that they wanted to have in the piece? Had they forgotten that something still needed to be corrected?

### Sharing and/or Publishing

**Acknowledging and celebrating the writing.**

At this stage, there are many ways to acknowledge and celebrate students' writing efforts. Sometimes the work is read to our class using an "author's chair" or read to other math classes. Sometimes it is more appropriate to display the papers on the wall. Another idea is to compile a class book including all the pieces and have the individual authors also create illustrations.

## The Writing Process in Action

As a way to best illustrate the integration of math writing with the writing process, let me share a few activities that have proven successful in the classroom. These activities are very simple, but the steps or stages of the writing process can be incorporated to extend the type of writing and research that students produce to satisfy the requirements of the *Common Core State Standards*.

### Mystery Number

The assignment begins first with an explanation of the writing students are to generate. They are to choose any number, independently research the number, and write a piece in which they never directly identify the number by name to see if someone can guess the number from their writing. Students are encouraged to think about it as a short scenario or imaginary situation in which by recounting it, they end up describing their number.

> **Mystery Number Prompt**
>
> Create an imaginary situation in which you end up describing and revealing characteristics of any number you choose, but you can never actually tell the reader what number it is. They have to guess what number it is from your description.

Once students have chosen their number, they use the *Thinking through Your Writing* activity sheet (Figure 4.1) to gather their ideas as part of prewriting. During a whole-group discussion, the class talks about and fills in the different items on the sheet.

**Topic:** Students place a question mark there so that their individual numbers would remain a secret.

**Purpose:** Here students re-examine examples that have been shared previously in class. We discuss how each of the examples is in first-person and also talk about the qualities of writing in first-person. Students write *to describe a number in a first-person narrative but without actually identifying it by name* on the prewriting sheet.

**Information Questions:** Having stated our purpose, students then brainstorm what sort of information might be best researched for this assignment. Their informational questions are then copied onto their individual sheets.

1. How many digits does my number have?

2. What is the sum of my number's digits?

3. Is my number a prime number, or can it be factored?

**Form:** Students decide whether this assignment should be written in paragraph form as opposed to a poem or list.

Students then use the completed *Thinking through Your Writing* activity sheet (Figure 4.1) as a guide during their research and note taking. Students choose to use books from the library or Internet resources to complete this research. The rest of the writing process ensues, and students share their paragraphs with others so they can guess what number is being described in each piece of writing.

---

### Mystery Number Student Sample

**Name the Number**

Can you imagine visiting Numberland? It's a very special place with numbers of all quantities. While I was visiting Numberland, I met a charming little number. It introduced itself, but now I can't remember its name. I'm so embarrassed! If I describe it, maybe I'll remember it. It had more than two digits but fewer than four. It was more than 100 but less than twice that amount. It's also known as a prime number, which means it can't be factored. I remember it saying it couldn't be divided by 2, 3, or any other number except for one and itself. If it's divided by 11, there will be a remainder of 2. It has consecutive digits that add up to 6.

So what's the name of the number?
(*123*)

---

## Add-an-Attribute Poem

A simple, yet highly effective pattern that students can use when researching and thinking about the attributes of a certain concept in math is called an *Add-an-Attribute poem*. This type of activity helps as they are learning to read and locate relevant information. *Add-an-Attribute* poems simply start with *A* or *An* as the first line, and the noun being described is added as the second line. Each successive line repeats the previous line and adds an attribute, hence, an *Add-an-Attribute* poem. This type of poem can be used to describe any mathematical concepts such as geometric figures, factoring, area, volume, measurements, or fractions.

One way this was enacted in the classroom was using geometric shapes as the subjects of the poem. Students were provided an *Add-an-Attribute Planning Sheet* (Figure 4.3). On their planning sheets, students included the name of their shape and recorded their research as they studied them:

- How many sides does it have?
- How many angles does it have?
- How many sides are equal length?
- Does it have any parallel sides?
- Are any of the angles congruent?
- What are the sides of the shape called?
- Other interesting facts?

Students filled out the sheet with a bulleted jot list:

- has four sides
- has four angles
- two sides are equal in length
- only two sides are parallel
- two angles are congruent
- two sides are called bases, and the other two are called legs

Using the information from their planning sheet, students then composed their poems. Finally, students had an opportunity to take their poems to other classrooms and, without giving away their last line, have other students guess what shape each student had researched.

**Figure 4.3** Sample Add-an-Attribute Poem Planning Sheet

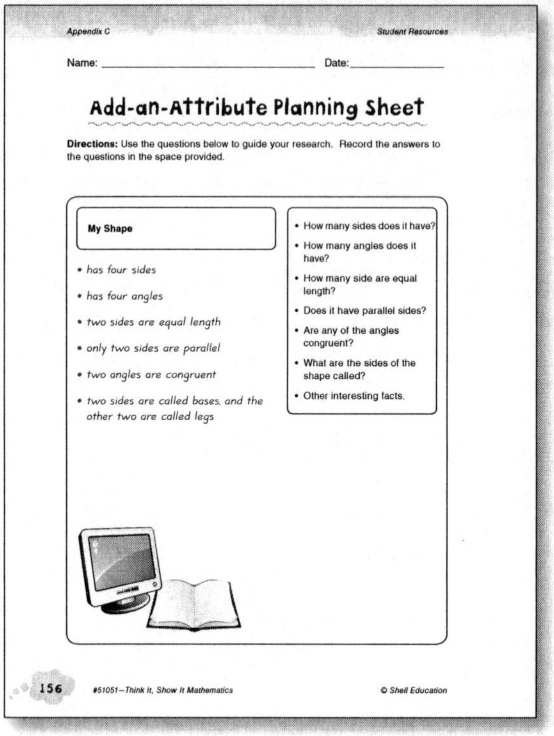

Appendix C — Student Resources

Name: _____ Date: _____

## Add-an-Attribute Planning Sheet

**Directions:** Use the questions below to guide your research. Record the answers to the questions in the space provided.

**My Shape** _____

- has four sides
- has four angles
- two sides are equal length
- only two sides are parallel
- two angles are congruent
- two sides are called bases, and the other two are called legs

- How many sides does it have?
- How many angles does it have?
- How many side are equal length?
- Does it have parallel sides?
- Are any of the angles congruent?
- What are the sides of the shape called?
- Other interesting facts.

156    #51051—Think It, Show It Mathematics    © Shell Education

Here is a student's poem best read aloud to get a feel for its poetic nature with the repetition.

## Sample Student Add-an-Attribute Poem

A

A shape

A geometric shape

A four-sided geometric shape

A four-sided quadrilateral geometric shape

A four-sided quadrilateral geometric shape with a pair of opposite parallel sides

A four-sided quadrilateral geometric shape with a pair of opposite parallel sides called bases

A four-sided quadrilateral geometric shape with a pair of opposite parallel sides called bases that are parallel and whose other sides are called legs

(*an isosceles trapezoid*)

Here is a student sample using a pyramid:

---

**Sample Student Add-an-Attribute Poem**

A

A shape

A geometric shape

A five-sided geometric shape

A five-sided geometric shape with a quadrilateral polygon for a base

A five-sided geometric shape with a quadrilateral polygon for a base and four faces

A five-sided geometric shape with a quadrilateral polygon for a base and four faces made of congruent triangles

What kind of shape am I?

(*a pyramid*)

---

Creatively bringing math writing into the writing class and making the most of the writing process helps students learn more about their math content and also supports their growth as writers. It helps them gain greater skill, control, and independence with their writing. Along with feeling more successful, it deepens students' understanding of the processes and functions of writing. They sense that they are becoming real math writers. Part of this emerging awareness of our "real writers" is their understanding of the different purposes and types of writing.

## Writing Purposes and Different Types of Writing

To help students understand the different purposes and types of writing that are important in math, I start by having them close their eyes to imagine their "dream car".

> *If you had all the money you would ever need, what car would you have in your driveway?*

When they have fully visualized all of its details and are totally enthralled by their imagined dream car, I say:

> *Now, drop the engine out. So what do you have now?*

After the chorus of moans, I go on to explain that they have, from all appearances, what looks like a fabulous car. It has wheels, doors, a stick shift, and every high-tech, computerized, luxury option possible, but it has no engine, no power. It won't go anywhere. It won't take them anywhere. It just will sit in the driveway and rust. The same is true with writing. I go on to say:

> *You can have words on paper—even correctly spelled words. You have properly indented, adhered to your margins, and included a title. So it looks like great writing, but writing has to have a motor. It has to be powered and have an objective. If it does not, it's just words without purpose written on paper. The words in your paragraphs have to accomplish something, such as describing an idea, explaining a procedure, or presenting a comparison of two or more subjects. Perhaps what the words need to do is persuade readers about an issue. If they don't, it is like the car that just "looks" like a car: a paragraph with no engine.*

In the same way that the engine powers a car, the purpose of the writing drives a paragraph. This discussion, of course, is a lead-in to an examination of the different purposes and types of writing. As a quick point of reference, different "types of writing" and different "genres" are actually addressing pretty much the same thing. Descriptive writing, as an example, is referred to both as a type of writing and as a distinct genre. For the sake of simplification and consistency in this section, I will use the terms *purpose* and *type*. The *Common Core State Standards* articulates it in this way:

"For students, writing is the key means of asserting and defending claims, showing what they know about a subject, conveying what they have experienced, imagined, thought and felt. To be college- and career-ready writers, students must take task, purpose, and audience into careful consideration, choosing words, information, structures, and formats deliberately" (2010, 63).

In math, the most common and effective types of writing include:

- narrative
- compare/contrast
- persuasive/argument (opinion)
- descriptive
- informational/explanatory and procedural

## Narrative

Narrative is text that tells a story by relating the events of an experience or story. The story can be real or imagined. Nonfictional experiences of writers presented as a story are most often referred to as "personal narratives."

These are some of the elements a writer uses to create a story:

- **Characters**: people, animals behaving like people, or inanimate objects presented with human characteristics in the story
- **Plot**: actions and events in the story and what the characters do
- **Dialogue**: spoken conversation between characters during the story
- **Setting:** specific time and place of the story
- **Exposition:** the background information on the characters and setting explained at the beginning of the story

A helpful graphic organizer for students to use when planning the sequence of a narrative is shown in Figure 4.4. A story map organizer appropriate for elementary students can be found in Appendix C.

**Figure 4.4** Plot Diagram

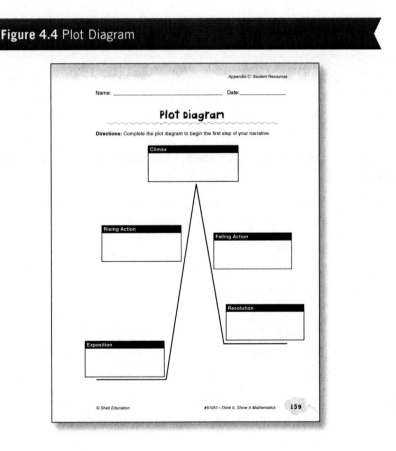

Along with the *Plot Diagram,* there are great story transition words and expressions for students to use to liven up their stories.

- And, as you've probably guessed by now,…

- Who would have guessed it when right then…

- And, as usually happens,…

- Then at that very moment…

- And it wasn't long before…

- Then, out of nowhere…

- And, lo and behold, right then…

- And wouldn't you know…

- But as time went on…

- Suddenly…

- But as luck would have it…

- Then, would you believe…

- Right after that…

- But sad as it may seem,…

In the final section of this chapter, I will discuss developing and using scoring rubrics. An example of a narrative is included on the Digital Resource CD. It would be helpful to share it with students as a model for them before they write their own narrative.

**Possible narrative math prompts include:**

- Create a short story in which a character must add the cost of five different items from a store and then use subtraction.

- Write an adventure or an action story involving exciting calculations with distance and time.

- Pick one standard of measurement (length, capacity, temperature, or weight). Write a humorous story relating what would happen if there were no standards of measurement in this area.

## Compare/Contrast

Compare/contrast text makes its subjects understandable by providing information that shows their similarities and differences and/or advantages and disadvantages. A helpful graphic organizer for students to use when planning a comparative essay is shown in Figure 4.5.

**Figure 4.5** Comparisons and Contrasts

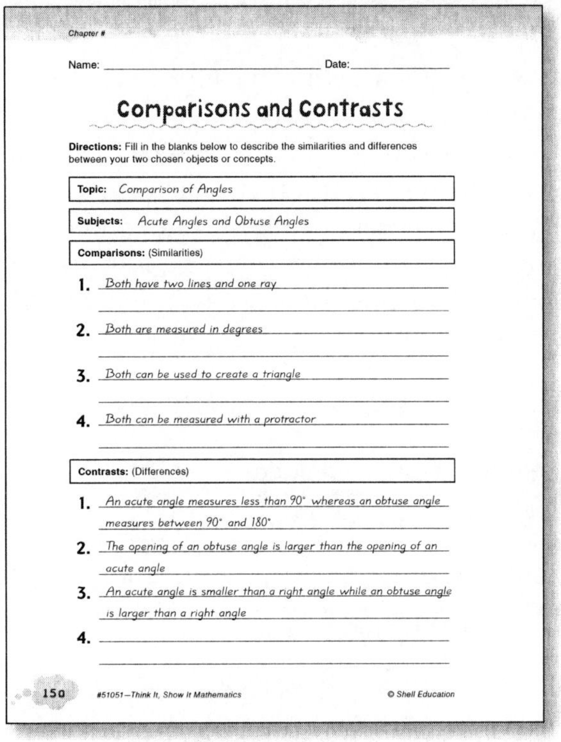

Chapter #

Name: ______________________ Date: ____________

Comparisons and Contrasts

**Directions:** Fill in the blanks below to describe the similarities and differences between your two chosen objects or concepts.

**Topic:** *Comparison of Angles*

**Subjects:** *Acute Angles and Obtuse Angles*

**Comparisons:** (Similarities)

1. *Both have two lines and one ray*
2. *Both are measured in degrees*
3. *Both can be used to create a triangle*
4. *Both can be measured with a protractor*

**Contrasts:** (Differences)

1. *An acute angle measures less than 90° whereas an obtuse angle measures between 90° and 180°*
2. *The opening of an obtuse angle is larger than the opening of an acute angle*
3. *An acute angle is smaller than a right angle while an obtuse angle is larger than a right angle*
4. ____________

150 #51051—Think It, Show It Mathematics © Shell Education

Even though the planning sheet has four lines for both the comparisons and the contrasts, students are not required to fill in each line. The accumulation of their research directs how much information they need. Frequently, they have needed more than four lines and have had to continue writing on the back of the sheet.

A list of words students can use when writing any text that needs to compare and contrast can be found on the next page.

### Words to Use When Comparing Different Subjects

- alike
- both
- as opposed to
- however
- yet

- rather than
- unlike
- different
- even though
- whereas

- in many ways
- likewise
- in the same way
- in contrast to
- compared to

Before students begin writing their own compare/contrast text, it is helpful to provide them with a mentor text. Mentor texts are written to explicitly model and highlight specific features of a type of writing for students. For example, in Appendix B a comparative mentor text includes the critical elements of a comparative text: subjects, topic, topic sentence(s), transition words, similarities and differences between its subjects, and words used to compare. By examining it in class and working together to identify the characteristics of the style of writing, students learn not only to identify the critical elements of comparative texts but also how a successful text that compares and contrasts might read.

### Possible compare/contrast math prompts include:

- Compare obtuse and acute angles.
- Compare the different types of graphs we have studied and used in class.
- Compare fractions, decimals, and percentages.
- Compare intersecting, parallel, and perpendicular lines.

## Persuasive/Argument (Opinion)

Persuasive/argument texts try to convince the reader of the writer's beliefs or opinions, or present a sound and logically supported argument on a particular topic or subject. The *Common Core State Standards* makes the distinction between writing to persuade and writing that puts forward a formal argument. Persuasive writing uses strategies such as appealing to the credibility, authority, or character of the writer to make its case to the reader, whereas a formal "argument" uses the logic and reasonability of the evidence it presents to make its case. For younger students, the *Standards* use the term "opinion" to refer to this developing purpose in writing (2010, 23–24). Specifically in mathematics, persuasive/argument writing supports the idea that all students should be able to "construct viable arguments and critique the reasoning of others" (2010, 6).

An easy formula to use with students when they write opinions can follow the pattern of opinion, reason, and restated opinion.

## Opinion, Reason, and Restated Opinion

### 1. Topic Question:

Begin with a topic question to focus your writing.

### 2. Opinion Sentence:

Write an opening sentence clearly stating your opinion (what you think). Use one of these sentence stems to start your sentence: *I think, I don't think, I believe, I don't believe, In my opinion.*

### 3. Reason Sentences:

Continue by writing two or more sentences with the different reasons you have for your opinion (why you think what you think). Use one of our transition words with each sentence: *first, second, also, next, finally, in addition, besides.*

### 4. Restated Opinion Sentence:

Finish by writing a sentence in which you restate your opinion (what you think) but try to say it in different words.

Here is an example:

Should the price of chocolate milk go up in the school cafeteria? What is your opinion? (*topic question*)

I don't think the price of chocolate milk should go up in the school cafeteria. (*opinion sentence*)

First (*transition word*), the new price will make it too expensive for students to buy it (*first reason sentence*). Also (*transition word*), it's already more expensive than the regular milk and more expensive than chocolate milk at other school cafeterias (*second reason sentence*). I think the cost of chocolate milk should stay the same (*restated opinion sentence*).

Evolving from this simple pattern, students follow their reason sentences with support sentences. Students learn that they can support their reasons by giving a fact, further explanations, or details.

> First, the new price will make it too expensive for students to buy (*reason sentence*). It would change from $0.75 to $1.50 (*support sentence*).

Although they are presented as reason sentences and support sentences, readers can easily see how students can learn to combine these two simple sentences into one complex sentence:

> First, the new price will make it too expensive for students to buy because it would change from $0.75 to $1.50.

Through this process, students learn that an effective opinion paragraph uses and follows this pattern:

## Question → Opinion → Reason → Support

Mathematical arguments are what I call *math-based persuasive text*s. These texts challenge students with trying to convince the reader of their beliefs or viewpoints through the powers of their personal persuasion and supported by facts and mathematical reasoning. This becomes what I term *opinions backed up by math*. I encourage students to rely on measured and thought-out logic rather than only emotion in their reactions to opposing viewpoints.

My instruction includes two planning frameworks for math-based persuasive texts: 1) Opposing Reasons/Your Argument, and 2) Topic, Issue, and Position Statements.

The first framework directs students to think through and anticipate opposing reasons of those who might have a different opinion or viewpoint. Students then develop the points of their counterreasoning—their arguments. The planning sheet used with this approach is shown in Figure 4.6.

**Figure 4.6** Opposing Reasons/Your Argument Planning Sheet

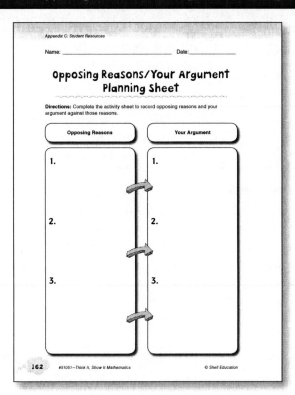

On the planning sheet, students list three possible opposing reasons (or more if needed) about the issue being addressed in their paper or discussion. Directly across from each opposing reason, they formulate and write their counterargument. With this, they need to consider math-based thinking such as:

- Are there factual or informational errors in the opposing reasoning?

- Are there drawbacks to a line of thinking?

- Is there an alternative explanation to one or more of their points?

Here is an example of a persuasive prompt that is best served by using the *Opposing Reasons/Your Argument Planning Sheet*:

**Prompt:** You have a friend who thinks math is not needed in school. Write a letter in which you try to persuade him or her to think differently.

Here is how a student began to develop the counterarguments of her letter.

| Opposing Reason | | Your Argument |
|---|---|---|
| Math is boring. | → | Math is only boring when you don't understand what's going on. |
| I will never use math. | → | Math is used in lots of things, like budgets, calculating tips, sale prices, measuring, and gas mileage. |
| I can use a calculator if I need math. | → | Calculators will only give the right answer if you know the right numbers to input. |

When working on this type of text, it is important to teach students that there are two patterns of rebuttal that they can use when presenting their argument. The first is where all the opposing reasons are explained and summarized before the writer presents his or her point of view or counterarguments. The second pattern is where the writer addresses each opposing reason sequentially and individually, one point at a time. When using either of these patterns, students can pick among these sentence stems and phrases to help them develop and write their argument:

- I realize you → believe, feel, maintain, want, favor, support, argue, make the case/point

- I understand you → believe, feel, maintain, want, favor, support, argue, make the case/point

- Even though you → believe, feel, maintain, want, favor, support, argue, make the case/point

- Although you → believe, feel, maintain, want, favor, support, argue, make the case/point

- But, Yet, However, I question, On the other hand, Nevertheless

In the preceeding example addressing whether math is needed in school, students utilized the *Opposing Reasons/Your Argument Planning Sheet* (Figure 4.6) to write an informal letter. The criteria used for evaluating the content of their letters is shown below:

Your letter will be scored on how well you:

- Clearly state your position on the issue.

- Accurately anticipate and address your readers' concerns and points of view opposing your position.

- Describe the points in support of your position, including examples and other evidence.

- Write in a friendly and engaging style.

There are two mentor texts connected to this assignment in Appendix B.  One text models the pattern of rebuttal where the opposing reasons are first explained and summarized before the writer's counterarguments are presented.  The other example models how each opposing reason can be refuted sequentially and one point at a time.

While the assignment in this example was an informal letter, students could have been asked to produce a more formal persuasive essay instead on different topics and issues. Here is a basic outline to help students in structuring a persuasive/argument essay.

**Begin (Introduction):**

- Engaging topic sentence(s)
- Question, Quote, or Surprising/Emotional Statement
- Concise explanation of the issue
- Clearly stated writer's position on the issue
- Helpful words and phrases:

  - In my opinion
  - I believe
  - It is my belief that
  - From my point of view

  - I question whether
  - I (dis)agree
  - I maintain that
  - There is no doubt that

**Continue (Body of the essay):**

- Mathematical reasons or arguments to support the writer's position while addressing possible opposing positions
- Examples, illustrations, logic, and/or mathematical evidence to support each of the writers points
- Helpful words and phrases

  | | | | |
  |---|---|---|---|
  | first | last | although | similarly |
  | to begin with | consequently | despite | further |
  | next | in addition | on the other hand | for example |
  | because | according to | still | in fact |
  | since | I believe | I personally believe | as evidence |
  | for example | in my opinion | | for instance |
  | finally | in my experience | moreover | in support of this |
  | | | besides | |

**Finish (Conclusion)**

- Restatement of the issue and the writer's position (try not to use the exact wording you used in your introduction).

- Reiteration of key or most powerful points of writer's reasons or arguments (again trying not to use the same wording used in the body of your essay).

- Ending with a strong summarizing statement(s), possibly making a powerful personal or emotional appeal.

- Helpful words or phrases

  - to sum up
  - in short
  - in brief
  - as you can see

  - as I have explained
  - in summation
  - in other words

  - in conclusion
  - in any event
  - as I have noted

  - obviously
  - as you can see
  - without a doubt

To prepare for an essay of this nature requires that during thinking and research, students clearly identify the topic, the issue, and their position on the given issue; select relevant background information, and finally—and most importantly—develop reasons to support their position. The *Topic, Issue, and Position Statement Planning Grid* is used to document this thinking and research (Figure 4.7).

**Figure 4.7** Topic, Issue, and Position Statements Planning Grid

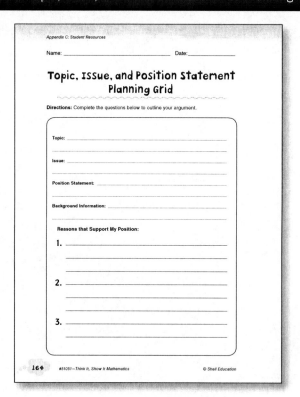

The following planning grid presents a more useful prewriting strategy when the concept or issue being addressed has multiple answers or cannot be answered with a clear-cut yes or no. Many real-life math scenarios are not that black and white and require the student to address and wrestle with multiple sides to a problem. For example, there are many factors to consider when discussing how much homework should be assigned.

Notice how this student had to thoroughly consider both sides of the issue (Figure 4.8).

**Figure 4.8** Sample Topic, Issue, and Position Statement Planning Grid

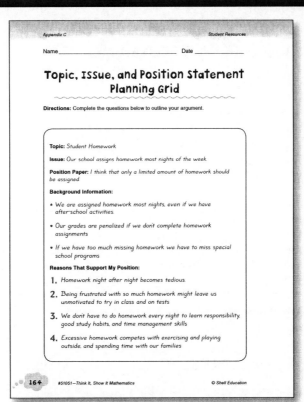

By thinking through each of the items on the planning grid, the student was not only able to connect prior knowledge with newly researched information but also to begin to formulate the points he or she would eventually want to make in the essay. During the composition process, he or she can use these familiar persuasive words and phrases.

### Topic Sentence and Position Stems:

- In my opinion
- I believe
- It is my belief that
- I question whether
- I (dis)agree

## Presenting New Information Words and Phrases:

- first
- second
- third
- finally
- last
- one way
- a second way

- another way (method, means, technique, approach, tactic)
- furthermore
- also
- in addition
- besides
- next
- moreover

## Phrases to Introduce Reasoning and Evidence:

- for example
- in fact
- for a case in point

- as evidence
- for instance
- in support of this

## Cause and Effect Words and Phrases:

- since
- because
- due to
- for this reason
- therefore

- caused by
- as a result of
- consequently
- leads to

- is responsible for
- in effect
- brought about
- made possible

### Possible persuasive math prompts include:

- You are responsible for buying drinks for your class party. One store has six-packs of 12-fluid-ounce cans of soda for $2.15, while another store has a special four-pack of 16-fluid-ounce bottles for $3.75. How would you mathematically persuade your class which of the stores offers the best deal?

- Michael doesn't believe he needs to learn his multiplication facts because he can always use his calculator. How could you persuade him that he will need to know his facts?

- Thomas didn't turn in two of his 10 homework assignments. His teacher said that anything less than 75% of homework papers completed and turned in would result in a loss of 20 points on the first-quarter grade. Should Thomas lose the 20 points? If you think not, how could you mathematically persuade his teacher that he shouldn't lose the points? A mentor text for a formal persuasive essay is included in Appendix B.

## Descriptive

Descriptive text accurately describes a person, place, thing, or concept by presenting a clear illustration of that person, place, thing, or concept. Effective descriptive writing in math is derived in part from two areas: descriptive imagery and content-specific word usage. In describing symmetrical figures and where they're found in the world around them, for example, students might want to include descriptive imagery with such ideas as what it looks like, what sounds can be heard, if any, if it has a certain smell, or its function. Along with this, students would need to use domain-specific words that are related to the topic. Here, for example, are some domain-specific words for symmetrical shapes:

- symmetry
- line of symmetry
- vertical
- horizontal
- diagonal
- balanced
- asymmetrical
- line symmetry
- reflectional symmetry
- axis of symmetry
- congruent parts

The *Descriptive Writing Planning Sheet* (Figure 4.9) can be used to help students plan for this type of writing. They identify their topic in the oval in the center, and as they research, they record nouns, verbs, and adjectives that are specifically related to their topic and might be used in their paper.

**Figure 4.9** Descriptive Writing Planning Sheet

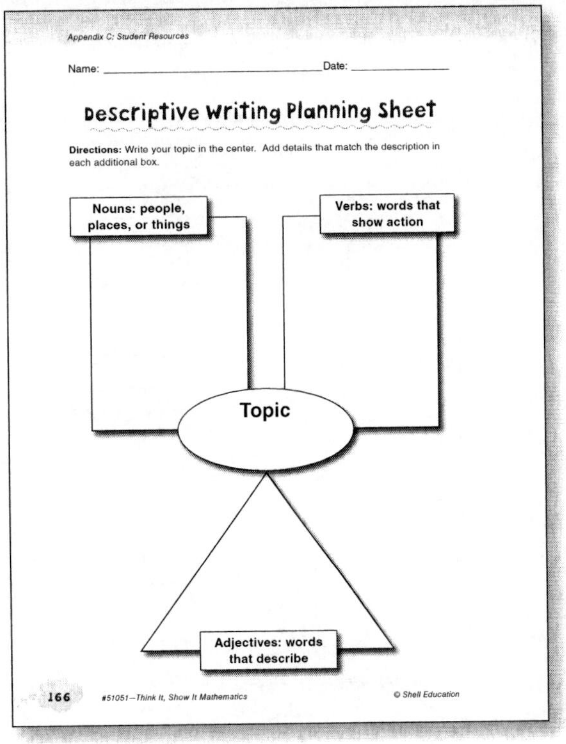
Appendix C: Student Resources

Name: ____________________ Date: __________

**Descriptive Writing Planning Sheet**

**Directions:** Write your topic in the center. Add details that match the description in each additional box.



166 #51051—Think It, Show It Mathematics © Shell Education

The goal is not necessarily for students to use each and every word in their paper or report but to have them available as they draft their paper. Furthermore, in order to use these words correctly in their piece, they will need an accurate understanding of the words' meanings in the context of their topic.

As an example, here are content words for a paper on measuring angles:

| **Nouns** | **Verbs** | **Adjectives** |
|---|---|---|
| • angle | • measure | • obtuse |
| • vertex | • line up | • acute |
| • ray | • rotate | • right |
| • degrees | • trace | • vertical |
| • protractor | | |
| • semicircle | | |
| • endpoint | | |
| • legs of angle | | |

The *Descriptive Writing Brainstorming Guide* (Figure 4.10) is an activity sheet to support descriptive writing that incorporates descriptive imagery. Here, students brainstorm details or images related to their topic, using as many of their senses as they can.

**Figure 4.10** Descriptive Writing Brainstorming Guide

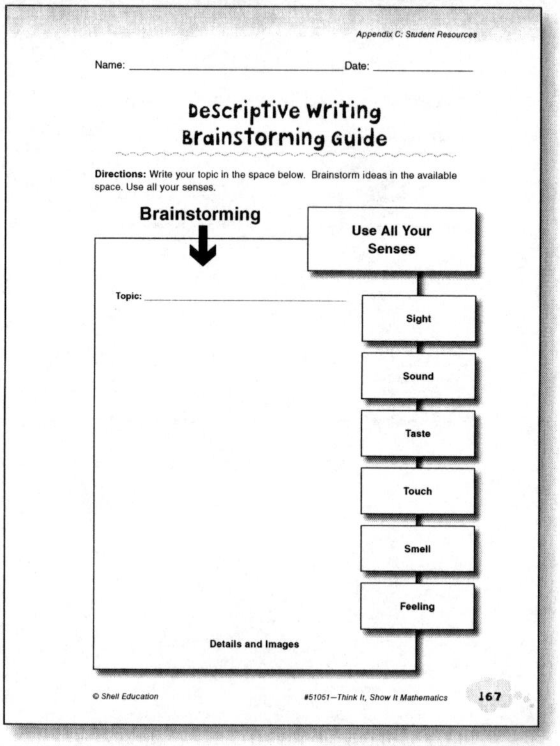

As an example, prior to working with a series of math activities and word problems centered around oranges, each student was given an orange. They were asked to describe it using their five senses. The description needed to include both qualitative and quantitative data. Students and I brainstormed what sorts of things they needed to be aware of in order to write a description of their oranges.

### Sight

- What shape is your orange? Can you compare its shape to something else? Does it have a certain color? Can you see anything that distinguishes your orange? Does it look like any other fruit you've eaten before?

### Sound

- What sound do you hear when biting into your orange? Does the sound remind you of anything?

### Taste

- What does your orange taste like? Are there different tastes with different parts of your orange?

### Touch

- How does your orange feel when you hold it in your hands?
- What measurements can you take of your orange when you hold it?

### Smell

- Describe the smell of the orange peel. Does it smell different from the rest of the orange? Does it smell different from other fruits you've eaten before? If so, how is it different?
- Does your orange have a distinct smell or scent?

### Feeling

- Does your orange stir up any feelings in you?
- How did eating your orange make you feel?

Using the brainstorming guide as a reference, students were to generate descriptive words and images:

- zesty
- citrusy
- juicy pulp
- orange-yellow
- carrot-colored
- rubbery skin
- shiny
- sweet
- pitted like moon craters
- fresh as a summer day

Finally, they could write a description of their orange. A mentor text for this assignment can be found in Appendix B.

**Possible descriptive math prompts include:**

- Describe a rectangular prism.

- Describe the data on a graph (or table) and what it means.

- Describe how fractions are used in your home.

- Describe how stores use percentages when items are put on sale.

- Describe how probability is used in everyday life.

- Interview your parents and have them describe how mathematics is used in their job(s).

## Informational/Explanatory and Procedural

Informational/explanatory and procedural texts explain their subjects or topics by conveying relevant information supported by facts and illustrations and are elaborated on by further explanations or reasons. An explanatory text is one that teaches the reader about its topic, but the exact sequencing of its information is not critical. A procedural text, on the other hand, also teaches or informs the reader about a procedure or process, but the correct sequence of its tasks or steps is critical.

### Informational/Explanatory Text

Essential to explanatory writing is the inclusion of relevant information or critical points along with supporting facts, illustrations, and further explanations or reasons. Students must focus on information and details—*information* being the major ideas or critical points and *details* being elaborations on the information through facts, illustrations, and further explanations or reasons.

The graphic organizers students use for planning their informational/explanatory texts include recognizable geometric shapes: a rectangle and a diamond—the rectangle being where they record information (or the major ideas or critical points) and the diamond where they record details that elaborate on information (facts, illustrations, or further explanations). Figure 4.11 is one planning sheet for explanatory text. It is modeled in a web format, with spokes stemming out from the topic. Figure 4.12 is the same idea, but it's formatted as a chart similar to an outline.

**Figure 4.11** Explanatory Text Planning Web

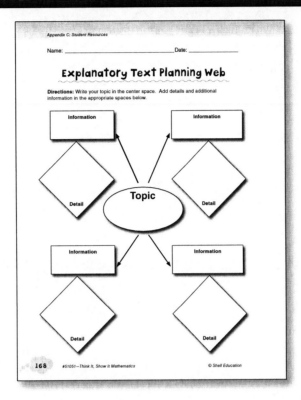

Using the graphic organizer seen in Figure 4.11 a student might, as an example, when preparing a report to explain what graphs are, identify one piece of information or point stating that there are many graphs that can be used to represent data.

**Information**

*Graphs are a way to show data that has been collected.*

And underneath the rectangle, have the following as an illustrating detail.

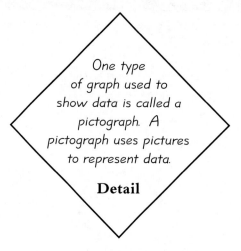

*One type of graph used to show data is called a pictograph. A pictograph uses pictures to represent data.*

**Detail**

Another diamond could include a second illustration of the example of the types of graphs used to explain data.

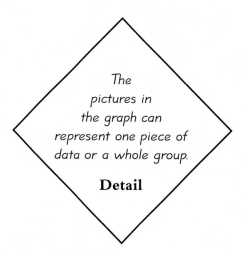

*The pictures in the graph can represent one piece of data or a whole group.*

**Detail**

Students are not limited to only one detail per piece of information simply because the graphic organizer shows only one diamond, nor in the same way, are they expected to only generate four pieces of information. The graphic organizer is a visual representation of the type of planning and research they are to record. As a habit, students need to think about the following: *What is the relevant information or critical points in my piece? How do I support or elaborate on them?* If more boxes are necessary to do this, students can use a second web or add on any open space of the planning sheet. Alternatively, students can use a large sheet of butcher or art paper to draw and fill in as many information rectangles and detail diamonds as dictated by their research. When students have more than one detail diamond under an information rectangle, we call those *dangling details*. Students like the alliterative ring of that expression.

With the same use of rectangles and diamonds, students use the design of the second graphic organizer (Figure 4.12) to list bullets as details under each of the information columns.

**Figure 4.12** Explanatory Text Planning Chart

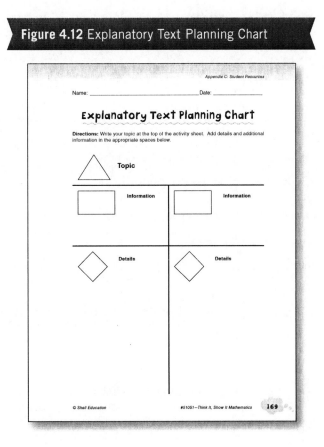

Here is a student sample on the topic of ratios:

| △ | **Topic:** Ratios<br>Ratios are comparisons between the quantities or number of two different things | | |
|---|---|---|---|
| ▭ | **Information**<br>Ratios can be written as words | ▭ | **Information**<br>Ratios can be presented as fractions |
| ◇ | **Details**<br>• 15 girls to 20 boys<br>• The order of the quantities is important<br>• They also can be shown using a colon 15:20 | ◇ | **Details**<br>• $\frac{15}{20}$<br>• 15 becomes numerator of the fraction, 20 is the denominator<br>• Fractions need to be reduced or simplied $\frac{3}{4}$ |

Both of these graphic organizers (Figures 4.11 and 4.12) function to help students record what they have learned about their topic and begin to organize their paper. A mentor text explaining ratios is included in Appendix B.

Possible explanatory math prompts include:

- Define or explain what a trapezoid is.
- Define or explain what a fraction is to someone who has never heard of or seen a fraction.
- Define or explain square root as it should be explained in a math textbook.

## Procedural Texts

Procedural texts are also an important type of writing in math. They primarily are used to give instructions or reiterate the steps of a mathematical procedure. A good example of a procedural text would be the sequencing of the steps followed in an algebra problem.

To prepare for this type of writing, students use the *Procedural Texts* activity sheet as shown in Figure 4.13. Here, students begin by identifying their topic and then writing an introductory sentence. From there, they write out each step of the procedure they are covering, using the transition words found at the bottom of the sheet.

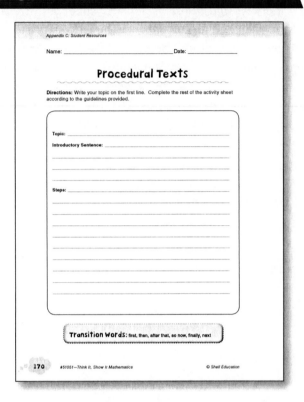

**Figure 4.13** Procedural Texts

Here is a student sample on the topic of mean.

## Topic: Mean

**Introductory Sentence:** Did you know that the mean of numbers is their average?

**Steps:** First, find the sum of all the numbers in a group. For example, the sum of 300 + 250 + 375 + 140 + 218 + 337 equals 1,620. Next, divide the sum by the number of addends, 1,620 divided by 6 equals 270. The mean of this set of data is 270.

## Justifying Procedures

As they did on their *Thinking and Justifying* activity sheet (Figure 3.5), students need to clearly explain their thinking and tell why they chose to explain a procedure in a particular way. In other words, they must be able to justify their steps. This is also an important aspect of the *Common Core State Standards for Mathematical Practice* (2010). To do this, students must be able to identify and create *what* statements and *why* statements within their writing. For example, *what* statements identify the mathematical operations that they used with the problem. *Why* statements explain why they needed to use these operations with specific references to contextual details from the text of the problem. Here are some examples:

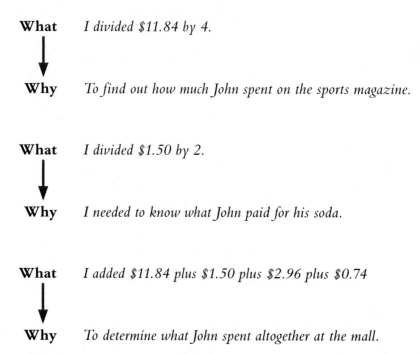

**What**     *I divided $11.84 by 4.*

**Why**    *To find out how much John spent on the sports magazine.*

**What**    *I divided $1.50 by 2.*

**Why**    *I needed to know what John paid for his soda.*

**What**    *I added $11.84 plus $1.50 plus $2.96 plus $0.74*

**Why**    *To determine what John spent altogether at the mall.*

## Try It!

An easy way to have students check to see if they included both the *what* and *why* statements in their writing is to have them underline them with colored pencils, the *what* statements in blue and the *whys* in red. Then, have students check by asking themselves *Do I have a red for every blue? A blue for every red? A what for every why? A why for every what?*

As students get more familiar with this type of writing, teachers can model more sophisticated sentence structure. For example, the *what* and *why* statements can easily be reversed by writing a complex sentence with a subordinate clause. When beginning sentences with the *why* statements, students can follow them with the *what* statements.

- Since I wanted to find out how much John spent on the sports magazine (why), I divided the $11.84 by 4 (what).

- Since I needed to determine how much John spent altogether (why), I added up all the items and found a total of $17.05 (what).

Ultimately, students should understand that in order to write procedural text that is both readable and logical, they should rely on five simple words: *since, because,* and *therefore, I know.* All students really need to remember is the following:

When writing *since,* use it at the beginning of a sentence:

**Since** John spent $11.84 on a new CD and $\frac{1}{4}$ of that amount on a sports magazine, I first divided $11.84 by 4.

When writing *because,* use it in the middle of a sentence:

I then added $0.75 with the rest of the items **because** I knew that $\frac{1}{2}$ of $1.50 equaled $0.75.

Use *Therefore, I know* when writing the final conclusion.

**Therefore, I know** that John spent a total of $17.05 while he was at the mall.

Some students may not be ready to jump into explaining and justifying their procedures in an open form such as is provided in the *Procedural Texts* activity sheet. Therefore, Figure 4.14 can be used as a scaffold to help them record the procedural steps they follow and justify each step through a written explanation. Teachers can model how to do this by projecting a transparency of displaying the sheet and using a think-aloud as they complete it. The left column of the organizer, titled *Tell what steps you did to solve the problem,* provides space to record the steps taken in the problem-solving process. Directly across from each step, in the column titled *Explain why you did the steps that you did,* record an explanation of the "why" behind each step should be recorded.

**Figure 4.14** What/Why Recording Sheet

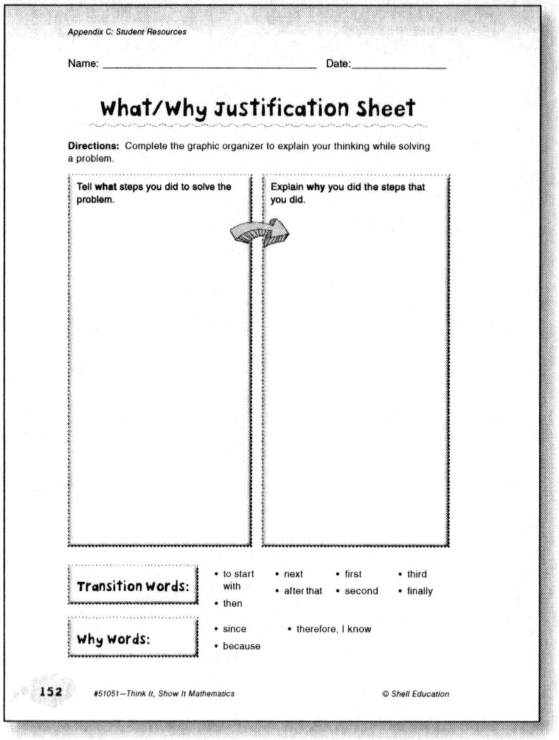

As students become comfortable in writing procedural text, they can use this activity sheet as a planning organizer to support the text they eventually record in *Procedural Texts*. This activity sheet can be projected and used as a group think-aloud resource.

### Possible procedural math prompts include:

- Explain the steps you used in solving this problem. (Provide a problem suitable for students at the intended grade level.)

- Explain how you could find out the average length of time that students in your class spend on homework each night.

- Sharon is 4 feet 6 inches tall. Vickie is 55 inches tall. Which girl is taller? Mathematically demonstrate the correctness of your answer.

- You are offered your choice of two-fourths of a pie or six-tenths of a pie. Assuming you like the pie, which would you choose? Explain how you would justify your answer mathematically.

Before I move on to share ideas on developing and using rubrics in order to score the different purposes and types of writing we have in math, it is important that I reiterate what the *Common Core State Standards* stress:

"Students need to know how to combine elements of different kinds of writing—for example, to use narrative strategies within argument and explanation within narrative" (2010, 63).

In other words, although I presented the different purposes and types of writing in this section as distinct purposes and types, in actuality, texts often overlap and need to coexist with one another within a piece. At times, an explanation very often requires a comparative analysis to better illustrate a point in its explanation, or an argument may need to employ descriptions as part of its evidence.

Along with the writing in which students are required to explain their mathematical thinking, an integrated and literacy-enhanced math program engages students with writing in all the different purposes and types of writing. Students come up with wonderful, creative stories with their narrative plots centered around a mathematical operation or concept, or perhaps where a mathematical process is personified in a story. They write math poems. They keep definitions of new mathematical (domain-specific) vocabulary words in math journals. They come to understand a new concept or idea by comparing it with and contrasting it to a familiar one. They refine their writing skills when required to produce a clear and coherent persuasive "argument" with support and mathematical evidence. In all of these endeavors, the act of writing helps students structure their thoughts and thereby solidify their mathematical understandings.

Equally valuable is the fact that by writing in their math classes, students transfer and support skills from one subject area to another. They learn that writing is one of their learning tools, not only in math and language arts but also in all of their subject areas. They no longer linger under the impression that writing is the exclusive property of the English teacher. No longer are they allowed to pose the question *This is math class, so do spelling and grammar count?* A visual representation that I present to students helps them see that writing in math is actually a combining of three distinct skills sets: mathematical skills, concepts, and principles are fused with language arts strategies for writing for different purposes and types of writing. Supporting the whole process is the precise use of the discipline-specific language and terminology of mathematics (see Figure 4.15).

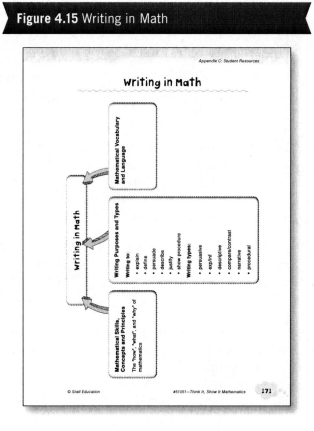

**Figure 4.15** Writing in Math

## Using Rubrics for Mathematical Writing

Assessment rubrics can be powerful learning tools. In a nutshell, rubrics are scoring guides for teachers (and students) to use in assessing and determining the overall quality of students' work. In mathematical writing, a rubric can be used to assess the following:

- quality of writing

- quality of math content

Rubrics provide the opportunity to directly evaluate students writing. They provide an analytical evaluation of student's work with specific, predetermined criteria, which are spelled out on the rubric and used to score students' work. As they are working on their text, students know what the criteria for their score will be. With rubrics, there is also a range of scores identifying both strengths and weaknesses of the work as opposed to there being one right or wrong answer or a single letter grade.

The rubrics I have developed to use in scoring students' writing in math are rooted in the traits of effective writing and are written to address the unique features of math writing. In developing each one, I addressed these conditions:

1. Is the math content complete, accurate, and contains no misconceptions?

2. Which purpose and type of writing are being addressed? What specific characteristics and elements of that purpose and type of writing do I want students to concentrate on?

3. How grammatically correct will students need to be?

4. How much should style (voice, word choice, and sentence fluency) play in my scoring of students' work?

In this effort, I designed the rubrics using three strands, each with its own point value. Here are the criteria for each strand:

1. **Content (Idea):** Overall clarity, accuracy, organization, and use of domain-specific vocabulary (0, 5, or 10 points):

Is the math content complete, accurate and contains no misconceptions?

Does the piece demonstrate an acceptable level of proficiency with its principle purpose and audience? If it is, for example, an informational/explanatory text, does it reveal the relevant information and/or critical points along with sufficient elaboration required with explanatory writing? Or does an argument piece present the required elements of persuasion? Has it needed to embed writing features of other types of writing, (e.g., an argument needing a comparative illustration)? Is it presented in a way that logically flows and connects one idea to the next? Does it use transitions effectively? Does its organization make it easy to follow and understand? Has the writer accurately and effectively included the vocabulary germane to the topic (domain-specific words)?

2. **Style:** Voice, word choice, and sentence fluency (0, 5, or 10 points):

These are the criteria that separate merely competent writers from writers that produce texts that are not only mathematically engaging and informing but also read comfortably.

- accurate and precise word choices with examples of figurative language (when appropriate)

- a variety of different sentence structures

- reads well out loud and is interesting to listen to

**3. Conventions:** Mechanical and grammatical correctness (0, 5, or 10 points):

An assessment of the student's correct use of English conventions:

- complete sentences where the subject and verb agree
- correct use of modifiers
- correct use of commas, apostrophes, and quotation marks
- abbreviations and capitals are used appropriately
- words are spelled correctly
- paragraphing aids readability

You may notice that the most points are assigned to the content strand. With writing in math, the writing must support the content and not the other way around. Accurate math remains the principle element with grammar and style playing an important but supportive role. Sample rubrics are included in Appendix D. These should be viewed as models and adapted to best meet your needs and the needs of your students.

Writing to further learning plays an essential part of math learning. It helps students not only to read more deeply into math, but to analyze, synthesize, and articulate mathematical information. It differs from other forms of writing that have been explored in this book in that it stresses writing as a means of constructing and thinking through knowledge instead of writing that is used to only communicate finished thought (as in writing to demonstrate learning). Bringing math into the writing classroom, leading students through the stages of the writing process, and using tools such a graphic organizers and rubrics merges literacy with math. It assists students in learning to account for their mathematical thinking, clearly present positions on issues, effectively explain a concept, and explore creatively the amazing world of math. It is learning at its best! The writing serves the learner within the context of the learning.

# Data: The Math and Science Connection

The *Common Core State Standards in Mathematics* incorporate the most effective models from around the country, and students are provided with the opportunity to explain to themselves the meaning of a problem and to look for entry points to its solution. Additionally, the standards allow students to justify their decisions as well as reason data analysis—making credible arguments that take into account the framework from which the data occurred.

Mathematics and science share many commonalities. As a result, math applications can be used to support science concepts. Science requires observation, comparison, measurement, communication, and data analysis. These are all skills that are also addressed in mathematics. To be successful in science, students must have a good grasp of mathematical concepts. We can think of science as the natural, real world application of math. Without math, scientists would find it impossible to apply their findings.

## Data Analysis

Data that is obtained through the different tools of observations and through conducted investigations needs to be organized and interpreted as an important element of scientific inquiry. Gathering their data by means of data tables and organized with bar, circle, and line graphs gives students a visual display or representation of what they have learned from their investigation. It allows them to determine the relationship of their data to the question they were investigating, to discover patterns, classifications, and comparisons within that data, and to inform their eventual interpretation of their outcomes. Being able to communicate this understanding by learning and using the appropriate scientific thinking and language is, of course, another integral part of our inquiry-based instruction.

Figure 5.1 introduces students to two different, yet critical types of data analysis sentences:

- a generalized statement giving the outcome or the interpretation of data (Data Interpretation: What I know)

- a follow-up statement or statements of supporting evidence obtained from the data (Evidence statement: How I know it)

The activity sheet can be used to generate these statements from whatever visual representation students have used to gather, organize, and represent the data (e.g., data table, bar graph, circle graph, or line graph). As is done with all the paragraph frames, I model its use for the whole class by displaying the page.

**Figure 5.1** Writing Data Analysis Statements

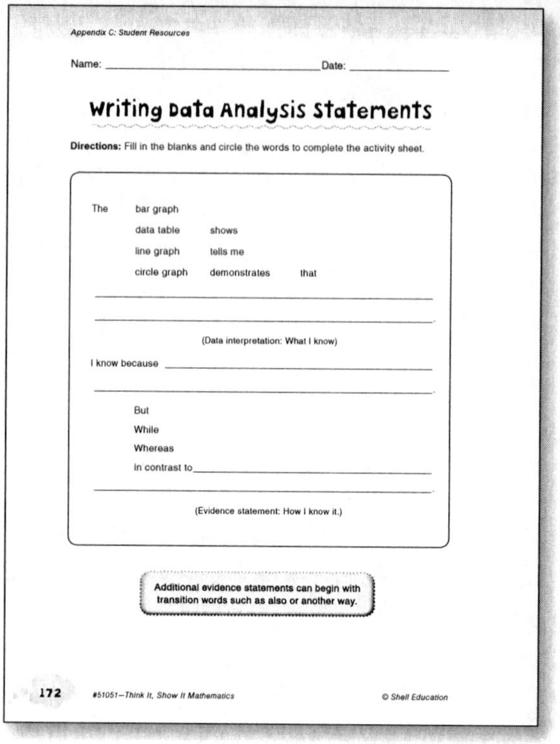

*Appendix C: Student Resources*

Name: _____ Date: _____

## Writing Data Analysis Statements

**Directions:** Fill in the blanks and circle the words to complete the activity sheet.

| The | bar graph | | |
| | data table | shows | |
| | line graph | tells me | |
| | circle graph | demonstrates | that |

_____

_____

(Data interpretation: What I know)

I know because _____

_____

But

While

Whereas

in contrast to _____

_____

(Evidence statement: How I know it.)

Additional evidence statements can begin with transition words such as also or another way.

To illustrate the data analysis statements students can produce, examples from different data tables and graphs are provided. Please note that in this section, I have purposely chosen to use simple examples in order to show you how data interpretation statements and evidence statements can be generated by students. You, of course, would be using investigations as dictated by your curriculum and classroom explorations.

## Data Tables

To practice writing data analysis statements, we conducted a simple experiment (Figure 5.2). This activity was adapted from the textbook *Teaching Science as Inquiry*. We made a ramp by placing one end of a plastic ruler on two stacked books and the other end of the ruler taped to the surface of the desk. At the end of the ruler where it was taped to the desk, we positioned a cup that we had cut vertically in half.

**Figure 5.2** Steel Ball Ramp Experiment Model

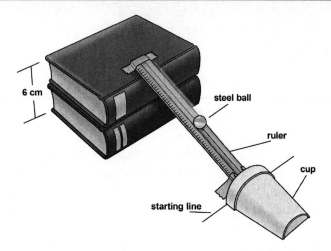

The experiment involved releasing a steel ball at different points along the ruler ramp and measuring how far the rolling steel ball would push the cup along the table. Before we started recording our data, however, we wrote our prediction statements.

*I predict _____ because _____.*

We conducted the experiment and recorded the results or data in a table.

| Distance steel ball rolled on ramp | Distance cup moved |
|---|---|
| 10 cm | 8 cm |
| 20 cm | 13 cm |
| 30 cm | 20 cm |

As a class, we used the *Writing Data Analysis Statements* activity sheet to write an analysis of the experiment. We started with a data interpretation statement and followed it with an evidence statement:

## Sample Student Data Analysis Statement

The data table demonstrates that the higher the steel ball is on the ramp, the farther the cup is moved. I know this because when it was rolled 30 cm, the cup moved 20 cm, while when it was rolled 10 cm, it only moved the cup 8 cm.

4th Grade Student

Notice that the data interpretation statements provide a generalized, qualitative analysis (more/less/most, longer/shorter, higher/lower, etc.) of the data, while the *evidence statements* give a quantitative breakdown of the measured data (30 cm, 10 students, 65 degrees). This is an important conceptual distinction for students as they move into more scientifically sophisticated investigations and inquiries.

The activity sheet's evidence statement forces students to make comparisons and present contrasts revealed by their data. Students often tend to give only a single piece of data with their evidence statements when using the steel ball on the ramp experiment, they might say, "because the cup only moved 8 cm when the steel ball rolled 10 cm." With this statement, only one piece of data is given. In order for the analysis to be scientifically valid, the contrasting data must also be given on how far the cup moved with the other lengths from which the steel ball was released. An important lesson when working with this activity sheet is to have students make their evidence statements include contrasting data much in the same way that they did with contrasting characteristics when writing contrast paragraphs. This is easily done, as the *Writing Data Analysis Statements* sheet (Figure 5.1) shows, by simply having them continue their statements to include their contrasting data by using the words *but, while, whereas,* or *in contrast to.*

### Sample Student Follow-Up Data Analysis Statement

The data table tells me that the steel ball needs to be let go higher up on the ruler to push the cup the farthest. I know this because it only went 8 cm when it rolled 10 cm, whereas when it rolled 30 cm, the cup went 20 cm.

4th Grade Student

To reinforce the importance and distinction between interpretation and evidence statements, have students color code their paragraphs, with their data interpretation statements highlighted in one color (e.g., red) and their evidence statements in a different color (e.g., green).

## Bar Graphs

Unlike data tables that collect and record numerical data (*the cup moved 13 cm when the steel ball was released from 20 cm*), bar graphs take the numerical data and display it, using rectangular columns. These bars can be presented vertically or horizontally, and each bar is proportional to the numerical value it represents. Bar graphs allow students to see differences and to make comparisons from their collected data. For example, when learning how to make and read a bar graph, students often record such things as the number of students in their class having certain eye colors. Here, in a type of data table referred to as a *frequency chart* or *frequency table,* is the data we recorded from my class. We then used the data to create a bar graph.

| Eye Color | Tally Marks | Frequency |
|:---:|:---:|:---:|
| black | ⦀⦀ || | 7 |
| green | ||| | 3 |
| blue | ⦀⦀ | | 6 |
| brown | ⦀⦀ ⦀⦀ | 10 |

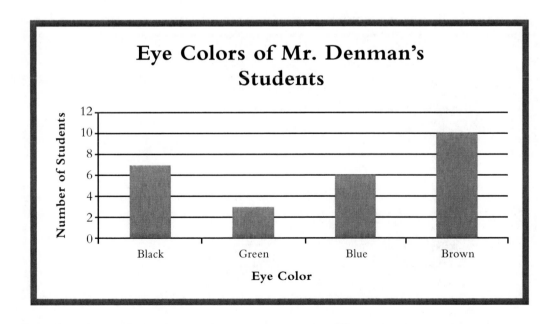

From the data collected and displayed on the bar graph, students produced written interpretation and evidence statements using the *Writing Data Analysis Statements* activity sheet.

### Sample Student Data Analysis Statements

The bar graph tells me that in Mr. Denman's class, most of the students have brown eyes. I know this because there were 10 brown-eyed students but only 7 with black eyes, 3 with green eyes, and 6 with blue eyes.

The bar graph demonstrates that more kids in Mr. Denman's class have brown eyes. I know this because there were 10 with brown eyes in contrast to only 7 with black eyes, 3 with green eyes, and 6 with blue eyes.

*3rd Grade Students*

Notice, as they did with their data tables, how students extended their evidence statements to include the contrasting data (*in contrast to only seven with black eyes, three with green eyes, and six with blue eyes*).

The activity sheet can also be used when students work with double-bar graphs or graphs that show data from two different sources. For example, if we wanted to compare the different eye colors of my class and my wife's class, the double-bar graph would look like this:

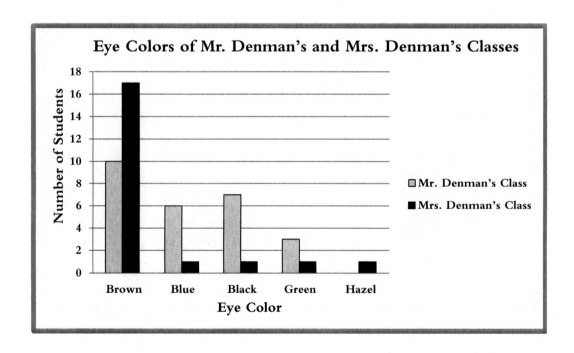

As they had with the single bar graph, students then can make data analysis statements.

---

### Sample Student Data Analysis Statement

The bar graph demonstrates that Mrs. Denman's class has more hazel eyes than Mr. Denman's class. I know this because Mrs. Denman's class has one person with hazel eyes while Mr. Denman's class has zero people with hazel eyes.

3rd Grade Student

---

A final element of the *Writing Data Analysis Statements* activity sheet can be seen in the following sample. Here, students are prompted to write additional statements simply by using the transition words *also* or *in addition*. As students become involved with more complex and multifaceted data, they often will need more than two statements to adequately present the analysis of their data. Notice how this student took his original two-sentence analysis and expanded it by supplementing an additional data interpretation statement and evidence statement:

---

### Sample Student Data Analysis Statement

The bar graph tells me that Mrs. Denman's class has more brown eyes than Mr. Denman's class. I know this because Mrs. Denman's class has 17 brown-eyed students, but Mr. Denman's class has only 10 brown-eyed students. In addition, the bar graph shows that Mr. Denman's class has more students with blue eyes. I know this because Mr. Denman's class had 6 blue-eyed students, whereas Mrs. Denman's class had only one student with blue eyes.

3rd Grade Student

---

## Circle Graphs

The circle graph is a circular chart cut by radii into segments (to look like individual pieces of pizza) representing numerical values. It requires students to have a conceptual understanding of fractions and percentages. Like the bar graph, it helps students see differences and make comparisons with their data (*there were more students with brown eyes than any other color in Mr. Denman's class*), but unlike the bar graph, it can go further and display the relationship of the parts (segments) to the whole (circle). Although we now know there were more brown eyes in Mr. Denman's class in comparison to the other colors, the bar graph doesn't tell us what fraction or percentage of the whole class had brown eyes. This kind of analysis is best displayed by means of a circle graph.

As another example, the circle graph below shows the percentage of the school day that each of the different subjects is studied.

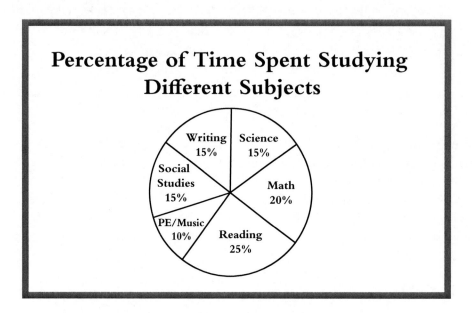

Looking at this graph and using the *Writing Data Analysis Statements* activity sheet, students wrote these analysis statements:

## Sample Student Data Analysis Statements

The circle graph shows that the largest percentage of our day is spent in reading. I know this because 25% of our day is reading, whereas all the other subjects are less than 25%.

The circle graph tells me that our longest subject is reading. I know this because reading is 25%, but math, science, writing, social studies, PE, and music are all less than 25%.

5th Grade Students

Here is another example from the circle graph in which the student has included an additional data interpretation and evidence statement using the transition phrase *in addition*.

---

### Sample Student Data Analysis Statement

The circle graph shows that the largest part of our day is spent in reading. I know this because 25% of our day is reading, whereas each of the other subjects is less than 25%. In addition, the circle graph shows that our shortest classes are PE and music. I know this because only for 10% of our day do we have PE and music in contrast to all the other classes that are longer than 10%.

5th Grade Student

---

## Line Graphs

Bar and circle graphs display data from tests and investigations that are fixed in time and space. For example, how many students have what color eyes on the specific day the survey was taken? It doesn't tell us how these numbers might have changed during the course of the year because of students moving and new students joining the class. How many students had brown eyes at the end of the year? How many had green eyes? Information that records changes over time can best be displayed using a line graph.

Along with interpreting both the bar and the circle graphs, students at the appropriate level are taught to create line graphs from the data they collect from their investigations. Here they need to be introduced to the concepts of independent variables (the "changed" variable, $x$-axis, or the horizontal line on the graph) and dependent variables (the "measured" variable, $y$-axis, or the vertical line on the graph).

A simple example is illustrated by the line graphs we created each school year to record the monthly amount of snowfall. We were interested in knowing what months received the most snowfall and what months the least, and how they compared from year to year. The progressing months from August through July, therefore, became our independent variable and the measured amount of snowfall each month was our dependent variable. We recorded monthly inches of snowfall as reported by our local newspaper on a chart that looked like this:

| Snowfall 2006 | | Snowfall 2007 | |
|---|---|---|---|
| **Month** | **Snowfall (in inches)** | **Month** | **Snowfall (in inches)** |
| August | 0 in. | August | 0 in. |
| September | 0 in. | September | 2 in. |
| October | 16 in. | October | 32 in. |
| November | 12 in. | November | 23 in. |
| December | 25 in. | December | 20 in. |
| January | 33 in. | January | 22 in. |
| February | 18 in. | February | 24 in. |
| March | 32 in. | March | 22 in. |
| April | 26 in. | April | 12 in. |
| May | 8 in. | May | 5 in. |
| June | 0 in. | June | 0 in. |
| July | 0 in. | July | 0 in. |

We constructed line graphs from our data.

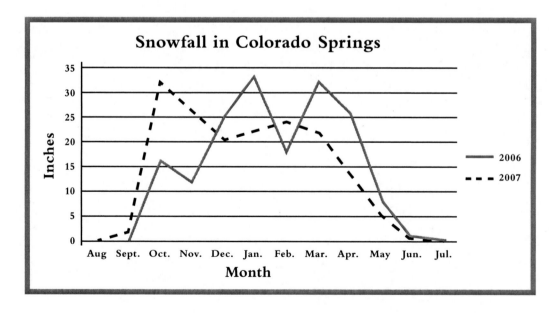

Using the information from the graph, students wrote data analysis statements. Here are two examples:

---

### Sample Student Data Analysis Statements

The line graph shows that January 2006 had the most snow. I know this because it had 33 inches of snow in contrast to all of the other months, which had less than 33 inches.

The line graph shows that June, July, August, and September in 2006 had the least snow. I know this because there was no snow recorded in either month, but all the other months had snow.

4th Grade Students

---

Notice again how these students used contrasting data with their evidence statements by using *in contrast to* or *but* and presented contrasting data from the graph.


## Scientific Conclusions (Arguments)

Foundational in the *Common Core State Standards* for writing is that students must be able to "write logical arguments based on substantive claims, sound reasoning, and relevant evidence" (2010, 1). Written scientific conclusions of students' investigations are in essence scientific arguments. Written explanations of their evidence along with the conclusions arrived at through their investigation function as scientific "substantive claims, sound reasoning, and relevant evidence."

Having students write data analysis statements while learning about data tables and bar, circle, and line graphs lays the groundwork for the longer conclusions that they will need to write with the investigations they conduct as they get older. Along with explanations that interpret and explain the outcomes of their observations and data, students will eventually be expected to go further with their written conclusions. Students will need to make reference to their hypotheses and whether the data confirm or refute them. Furthermore, their conclusions may require that they put forth an inference as to what caused the observed outcomes or perhaps pose an alternative and/or possible additional investigation. This level of detail and reasoning required to organize science experiences in language doesn't occur naturally in students. It is a needed skill that can be taught systematically.

To lay this foundation, it is important to begin by teaching students that a basic written scientific conclusion must start with their investigation question and contain four types of statements:

- answer statement
- evidence statement
- hypothesis statement
- conclusion statement

To illustrate each of these, let's take a look at a test item released by the Colorado State Education Department involving clay balls being launched from a spoon launcher.

## Task

Investigation Question: Does the size of a ball of clay affect how far it will go when launched from a spoon launcher?

To test Task #2, three pieces of clay were made into balls and launched from a spoon launcher. Each ball of clay was a different size. Each of the three balls was also launched three times and the distances they traveled were recorded by students on the table below.

**Distances the Balls of Clay Traveled**

| Ball Sizes | Trial 1 | Trial 2 | Trial 3 | Average Distance Traveled |
|------------|---------|---------|---------|---------------------------|
| small | 76 cm | 80 cm | 84 cm | 80 cm |
| medium | 50 cm | 42 cm | 46 cm | 46 cm |
| large | 8 cm | 16 cm | 12 cm | 12 cm |

## Investigation Question and Answer Statement

The design of any scientific investigation or investigation develops from the investigation question or what the student wants to discover or determine. For the investigation's conclusions to be valid, the data or evidence produced needs to specifically answer that question. We call this our *answer statement*. The answer statement, as it is aligned with *Common Core State Standards*, functions as the substantive claim of the scientific argument.

A technique to teach students when writing answer statements is to first identify the key words in the investigation question. Then, using those exact words, turn the question into an answer statement. For example, if we take the investigation question *Does the size of a ball of clay affect how far it will go when launched from a spoon launcher?*, we can identify and underline its key words:

*Does the <u>size</u> of a <u>ball of clay</u> <u>affect how far it will go</u> when <u>launched</u> from a <u>spoon launcher</u>?*

Then, we turn it into an answer statement that answers the question using the key words from the question:

*The size of a clay ball affects how far it will go when it is launched from a spoon launcher.*

Figure 5.3 shows the first page of *Writing a Scientific Conclusion*.

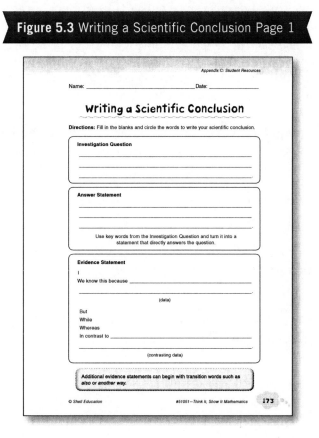

**Figure 5.3** Writing a Scientific Conclusion Page 1

## Evidence Statement

After writing their answer statements, students go on to support their answers by supplying evidence statements, which validate their conclusions. The sentence pattern is as follows.

*I/We know this because* _____ *but/while/whereas/in contrast to* _____ .
                                (data)                                                 (contrasting data)

*We know this because when the smallest piece of clay was launched, it went an average of 80 cm while the largest piece of clay only went an average of 12 cm.*

Notice how this evidence statement presented a piece of data from the chart, followed by its contrasting data. Students are taught to present one piece of data on their first lines and to continue with the sentence by giving its contrasting data. In addition, as students gain more practice in writing evidence statements, they are encouraged to give more than one evidence statement in their conclusions. By now, they have learned to simply use the transition words *also* or *another way* when presenting another piece of evidence.

Finally, referring to students' examples, you can see that their evidence was quantitative, or measured, and recorded data from the chart (*80 cm* and *12 cm* and *while the largest piece of clay only went an average of 12 cm*). Other evidence in another investigation or experiment, may require qualitative, or observed data. This can be written using the same sentence pattern. In the following example, we were observing how bar magnets interact:

### Investigation Question

Do the <u>different poles</u> (North and South) on <u>bar magnets</u> <u>determine</u> whether they <u>attract</u> or <u>repel</u> each other? (key words underlined)

### Answer Statement

The different poles on bar magnets determine whether they attract or repel each other.

### Evidence Statement

I know this because when I pointed a bar magnet at another bar magnet with the same pole, they repelled and moved away from each another, in contrast to when I pointed them with different poles and they were attracted and moved toward each other.

## Hypothesis Statement

This critical statement, as a part of a scientific conclusion, has students returning to their original investigation hypotheses and indicating whether they were confirmed or refuted. During the design of our investigations, students formulated their hypotheses in an if-then pattern:

*<u>If</u> size affects how far a clay ball will go, <u>then</u> the bigger the ball, the farther it will travel.*

The hypothesis statements that students use in their conclusions are written using the following pattern:

*This data/evidence refutes/confirms my/our hypothesis because* _____ .

*This data refutes my hypothesis because our experiment showed that the smaller balls traveled farther. I thought that since a larger ball would get more momentum, it would go farther.*

Since the hypothesis is not directly spelled out in the *Writing a Scientific Conclusion* activity sheet, the hypothesis statements students write must be written so that the reader of the conclusion will be able to know what the hypothesis was.

Equally, if not more important, students should try to articulate the reasoning behind their hypothesis statements, whether that reasoning is right or wrong. This, of course, is limited by the nature of the investigation itself and by the amount of background knowledge students bring to the task. Getting students into the habit of expressing reasoning promotes better scientific thinking. In addition, the inclusion of hypothesis statements makes their conclusions more complete by more accurately replicating the steps of the scientific method.

**Figure 5.4** Writing a Scientific Conclusion Page 2

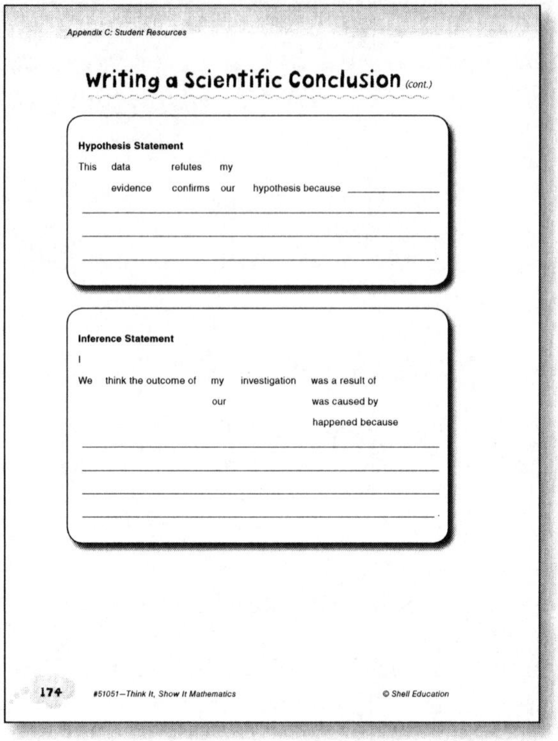
Appendix C: Student Resources

## Writing a Scientific Conclusion (cont.)

**Hypothesis Statement**

This data refutes my
evidence confirms our hypothesis because ____________
____________________________________________
____________________________________________
____________________________________________.

**Inference Statement**

I
We think the outcome of my investigation was a result of
our was caused by
happened because
____________________________________________
____________________________________________
____________________________________________
____________________________________________.

174 #51051—Think It, Show It Mathematics © Shell Education

An additional type of statement that augments both the evidence and hypothesis statements as well as prompts extended scientific thinking is called an inference statement. In inference statements, students formulate an inference as to why the data or test results turned out the way they did. Below is the sentence pattern with an example of a group's response.

I my
We think the outcome of our investigation was a result of
was caused by
happened because ________________.

### Sample Student Inference Statement

We think the outcome of our investigation was a result of weight and gravity. The larger clay ball was heavier than the smaller ball, so it took more force to move it the same distance. Since the clay balls were all launched with the same force, we now know that the heavier ball would not go as far.

7th Grade Student

## Conclusion Statement

The conclusion statement of a scientific conclusion might best be described as an *evidence-based learning statement*. The answer statement is an opening statement that directly answers the investigation question posed in the experiment. The evidence, hypothesis, and inference statements are statements presenting evidence supporting the answer statement as well as broadening and refining the scientific reasoning involved in the process. The conclusion statement, then, is a statement of what students now know or have learned as a result of the investigation (Figure 5.5). The conclusion statement is written in the following pattern.

Therefore,    I
In conclusion, we now know _____.

---

### Sample Student conclusion Statement

Therefore, we now know that the lighter the tissue paper ball is, the farther it will go when launched with the same force. In addition, we now know that the heavier the ball is, the shorter the distance it will go.

In conclusion, we now know that the heavier an object is, the shorter the distance it will travel when launched with the same force.

6th Grade Student

---

**Figure 5.5** Writing a Scientific Conclusion Page 3

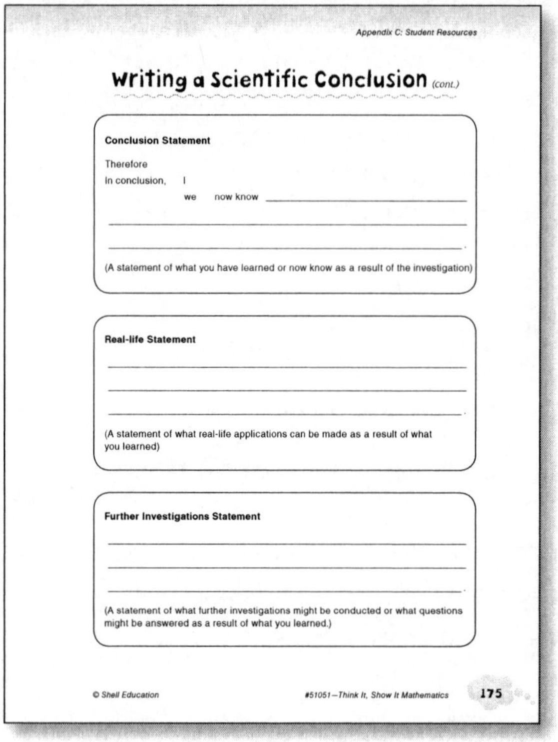

## Writing a Scientific Conclusion (cont.)

**Conclusion Statement**

Therefore
In conclusion,    I
               we    now know _____

_____

_____ .

(A statement of what you have learned or now know as a result of the investigation)

**Real-life Statement**

_____

_____

_____ .

(A statement of what real-life applications can be made as a result of what you learned)

**Further Investigations Statement**

_____

_____

_____ .

(A statement of what further investigations might be conducted or what questions might be answered as a result of what you learned.)

© Shell Education                    #51051—Think It, Show It Mathematics    **175**

There are two additional ideas that you may want to have students address in their conclusions. One asks them to think of or imagine any real–life applications of what they learned in the investigation. In other words, does knowing that a smaller object can be launched farther than a larger one when using the same force and under the same conditions apply to anything going on around us? Here, students have to think outside the box. These statements are referred to as *real-life statements*.

### Sample Student Real-Life Statement

I think from our conclusion that if I am in a snowball fight and my opponents are far away from me, I will need to make smaller snowballs if I want to hit them. However, if they are closer, I can make larger snowballs because I can use the same amount of force to throw them.

6th Grade Student

A final type of statement students can include with their conclusions is one in which they suggest what investigations or questions might follow as a result of what they have learned. This is identified as a *further investigations statement*.

```
Sample Student Further Investigations Statement
```

It might be interesting to see if the shape of the launched object would affect how far it travels. Would a round-shaped object go farther than a flat object?

Our group would like to determine whether, if we had the same size and shape objects, the length of the arm of the spoon launcher would have an effect on the distance each traveled.

6th Grade Student

Depending on the investigation being conducted and the level of experience your students have had in writing scientific conclusions, you may want to give different groups of students different criteria and investigations for their written conclusions. For example, you may want some students to write employing only a five-sentence conclusion paragraph with an investigation question, an answer statement, an evidence statement, a hypothesis statement, and a conclusion statement. Other students should be expected to write paragraphs that also include inference, real-life, and further investigations statements. Eventually, all students should be expected to write all of the different statement types in their mathematical conclusions. Appendix B includes an annotated scientific conclusion mentor text of a popular student investigation from the *National Center for Educational Statistics* (2000). It highlights each of the types of questions and statements used in scientific conclusions.

Mathematically-empowered students in the making are learners who have to monitor their own learning in order to continually appraise it. What they need to focus on is what will make whatever they are doing better the next time. Mastery will always, and only, be achieved through repeated practice, specific feedback, and incremental steps forward. If students are to be empowered by our instruction, it will be because they can use the skills we are teaching them confidently and successfully on another day, perhaps in uniquely different circumstances or contexts. It isn't enough for them to be able to construct a written explanation of a mathematical process in the classroom. They need to be able to use and apply that expository skill in other arenas on other days.

By being presented with a systematic approach to addressing word problems, an easy, fail-safe technique for constructing their written responses, and numerous ongoing classroom activities and routines to support learning, students dig deeper into their thinking and understanding. Perhaps it is best stated by this maxim:

Good writing requires good thinking;

Better writing promotes better thinking.

# References Cited

Bass, Joel, Arthur Carin, and Terry Contant. *Teaching Science as Inquiry,* 11th edition. 2005. New Jersey: Pearson Prentice Hall.

Bingham, Janet. "The Math Challenge: More thank Half in Test Fall Short." *The Denver Post,* March 3, 2000.

Gojak, Linda. 2011. *What's Your Math Problem? Getting to the Heart of Teaching Problem Solving.* Shell Education.

"Half of Fifth Graders Mastering Math." *Pueblo Chieftain.* March 3, 2000.

National Mathematics Advisory Panel. 2007. *Foundations for Success: The Final Report of the National Mathematics Advisory Panel.* Washington, DC: U.S. Department of Education.

National Center for Educational Statistics. (2000) 2006. *Released Item 4th Grade National Assessment of Educational Progress.* Virginia.

National Council of Teachers of Mathematics (NCTM). 2000. *Principles and Standards for School Mathematics.* Reston, VA: National Council of Teachers of Mathematics. Feb. 2008.

National Governors Association Center for Best Practices, Council of Chief State School Officers. 2010. *Common Core State Standards.* Washington, DC: National Governors Association Center for Best Practices, Council of Chief State School Officers. http://www.corestandards.org.

Smith, Frank. (1982) 2008. *Writing and the Writer.* New York: Teachers College Press.

Unit of Student Assessment, Colorado Department of Education. 2001. *2000–2001 CSAP Demonstration Packet: Math Grade 8, 19–20.* http://www.cde.state.co.us/assessment/documents/released/RE01ma8.pdf

_____. 2004. *2003–2004 CSAP Demonstration Packet: Math Grade 5, 1.* http://www.cde.state.co.us/assessment/documents/released/2004CSAPRelItems-Anchors_Gr5-10Math.pdf

_____. 2005. *2005–2006 CSAP Demonstration Packet: Math Grade 5, 18.* http://www.cde.state.co.us/assessment/documents/released/sci_demo_g5_2005.pdf

Van de Walle, John A. 2009. *Elementary and Middle School Mathematics, Teaching Developmentally,* fifth edition. Boston: Pearson.

Weber, Brian, and Holly Kurtz. "Half of Fifth-Graders Fail Math Test: Education Experts Say First-Year CSAP Scores Low Before Students Adjust." *Rocky Mountain News.* March 3, 2000.

# Scientific Conclusion

The mentor text below is annotated to support you during instruction. The student version of this text is provided on the Digital Resource CD (mentortext1.pdf).

**Investigation**: Two large mason jars are filled with equal amounts of water. One of the jars is painted completely black while the other is painted completely white. The temperature of the water is taken first thing in the morning and then each jar is left uncovered outside on a hot sunny day. At the end of the day the temperature is again taken.

**Investigation Question**: Is heat absorbed and/or reflected differently by different colors?

**Conclusion to Our Experiment**

Heat is absorbed and reflected differently by different colors [**answer statement**]. I know this because the temperature of the jar painted black rose four degrees while the white jar's temperature only rose two degrees [**evidence statement**]. Also, I know this because when I touched the black jar it was hot in contrast to the white jar, which was only warm [**additional evidence statement**]. This data refutes my hypothesis because I had predicted that it would not make a difference [**hypothesis statement**]. I thought what would make a difference was whether or not the jars were covered, like what happens when you leave car windows up on a hot day. I think the outcome of my investigation was caused by the sun's heat being absorbed by the black jar while being reflected by the white jar [**inference statement**]. In conclusion, I now know that the color black absorbs heat while the color white reflects heat [**conclusion statement**]. This explains why we wear white in the summer to stay cooler [**real-life statement**]. I wonder if we would discover the same thing if the jars were clear, but one was filled with black water and the other with white water [**further investigations statement**].

## Annotated Mentor Text: Scientific conclusions

Demonstrating investigation question, answer statement, evidence statements, hypothesis statement, inference statement, conclusion statement, real-life statement, and further investigation statement

# Acute and Obtuse Angles

The mentor text below is annotated to support you during instruction. The student version of this text is provided on the Digital Resource CD (mentortext2.pdf).

Two types of angles used in geometry are acute and obtuse angles [**topic and subjects**]. Although they are similar in many ways [**words used to compare**], there are, however [**transition word**] important differences between [**words used to compare**], acute and obtuse angles [**subjects and topic sentence**]. To begin with [**transition words**], both acute and obtuse angles have two lines or rays that share a common point called a vertex [**1st similarity**]. They are both measured in degrees [**2nd similarity**]. In addition [**transition word**], obtuse and acute angles are alike [**words used to compare**] because both can be used to create a triangle [**3rd similarity**]. Furthermore [**transition word**], an acute angle creates an acute triangle, and an obtuse angle makes up an obtuse triangle [**4th similarity**]. Similarly [**word used to compare**], both angles can be measured with a protractor and compass [**5th similarity**].

In contrast [**words used to compare**] the biggest difference between [**words used to compare**] acute and obtuse angles is their measurement. An acute angle will measure less than 90° [**1st difference**]. On the other hand [**words used to compare**], an obtuse angle measures between 90° and 180° [**2nd difference**]. This means that the opening of an obtuse angle is wider than the opening of an acute angle [**elaboration on 2nd difference**]. Finally [**transition word**], an acute angle has a measure or is smaller than a right angle, but an obtuse angle has a larger measure or is larger than a right angle[**3rd difference**].

### Annotated Mentor Text: Comparative

Demonstrating topic, subjects, topic sentence, transition words, similarities and differences between subjects, elaboration, and words used to compare.

# Letter 1

The mentor text below is annotated to support you during instruction. The student version of this text is provided on the Digital Resource CD (mentortext3.pdf)

Hi Sam,

I've heard that you're not a fan of math. You're not engaged in math class and don't understand its purpose. I maintain [**persuasive sentence stem**] that math is very important and will prove to be useful to you because math is full of necessary skills for your everyday life [**topic, issue, and position**]. Furthermore [**transition word**], as your friend, I need to tell you that many of your arguments are unfounded.

To start with [**transition word**], you think math is boring [**1st opposing reason**]. There isn't anything about your math class that you find interesting [**elaboration**]. You probably find it boring because you don't understand what's going on in class [**1st argument**]. It's normal to be uninterested in something if you're not very good at it [**elaboration**]. Fortunately, it's never too late to improve your math skills. There are many people willing to help you understand math [**further elaboration**]. Besides [**transition word**], you can't expect math class to be fun every day [**further elaboration on a point**]. Even though [**persuasive sentence stem**] you think that you will never use math [**2nd opposing reason**], the reality is that it is used in lots of things [**2nd argument**]. Math helps people stick to their budget [**elaboration**]. Math helps us figure out how much we should tip the server at a restaurant [**further elaboration**]. Math is also helpful to figure out the price of sale items at the mall [**further elaboration**]. My parents find it very helpful when they're trying to measure objects or when they're calculating gas mileage for a road trip [**further elaboration**]. Finally [**transition word**], I know [**persuasive sentence stem**] that you say you can use a calculator [**3rd opposing reason**], but it can't figure out how to work a problem for you [**3rd argument**]. Calculators only give you a correct answer if you know the right numbers to input [**elaboration**]. I realize that math may not always seem fun, but without it you would be lost [**concluding sentence**].

Your friend,

Maria

## Annotated Mentor Text: Persuasive Letter #1

(Each opposing reason refuted sequentially and one point at a time)
Demonstrating topic, issue, position, opposing reasons and arguments, transition words, elaboration on a point(s), and persuasive sentence stems

# Letter 2

The mentor text below is annotated to support you during instruction. The student version of this text is provided on the Digital Resource CD (mentortext4.pdf).

Hi Elizabeth,

I've heard that you're not a fan of math. You're not engaged in math class and don't understand its purpose. I maintain [**persuasive sentence stem**] that math is very important and will prove to be useful to you because it is full of necessary skills for your everyday life [**topic, issue & position**]. Furthermore [**transition word**], as your friend, I need to tell you that many of your arguments are unfounded. To start with [**transition words**], you think math is boring [**1st opposing reason**]. There isn't anything about your math class that you find interesting [**elaboration**]. You also say that you believe that you will never use math [**2nd opposing reason**]. Finally [**transition word**], I know [**persuasive sentence stem**] you believe that you can simply use a calculator [**3rd opposing reason**].

These ideas simply don't ring true. You may see math as boring, but you may feel this way because you don't understand what's going on [**1st argument**]. It's normal to be uninterested in something if you're not very good at it [**elaboration**]. Fortunately, it's never too late to improve your math skills. There are many people willing to help you understand it [**further elaboration**]. Besides [**transition word**], you can't expect math class to be fun every day [**further elaboration**]. Although [**persuasive word**] you believe [**persuasive sentence stem**] that you will never use math [**2nd opposing reason**], the reality is that it is used in lots of things [**2nd argument**]. Math helps people stick to their budget [**elaboration**]. It helps us figure out how much to tip a server at a restaurant [**further elaboration**]. It is helpful when you're figuring out the price of sale items at the mall [**further elaboration**]. My parents find it helpful when they're measuring objects or calculating gas mileage for a road trip [**further elaboration**]. Finally [**transition word**], a calculator can help you determine an answer, but it can't figure out how to work a problem for you [**3rd argument**]. Calculators only give you a correct answer if you know the right numbers to input [**elaboration**]. I realize that math may not always seem fun, but without it you, will be lost [**concluding sentence**].

Always your friend,

Alberto

## Annotated Mentor Text: Persuasive Letter # 2

(Opposing reasons first summarized and then refuted)
Demonstrating topic, issue, position, opposing reasons and arguments, transition words, elaboration on a point(s), concluding sentence, and persuasive sentence stems

# Homework

The mentor text below is annotated to support you during instruction. The student version of this text is provided on the Digital Resource CD (mentortext5.pdf).

Did you know that what you have to do most evenings is the result of a satellite launched in 1957? I am talking about homework, of course [**topic and topic sentence**]. There was once a state law abolishing it. In 1957 the Russians launched the first satellite into space. It was called *Sputnik*. The U.S. was afraid that American students weren't going to be able keep up with their Russian counterparts. The solution: Thrust tons of homework on American students so they would keep up [**issue**]. But earlier in 1901 in California there was a law passed outlawing homework [**continuing examination of the issue**]. How great would that be? Well, this isn't 1957 or 1901 and I maintain [**position sentence stem**] that there can be a balance between tons of homework every night and no homework at all [**position on the issue**].

Let's get the facts straight first. We are assigned homework most nights, regardless of other obligations we may have; our grades go down if we don't complete it, and students with too much missing homework aren't allowed to participate in special school programs [**issue**]. What is the reason behind all this? Practice makes perfect [**1st opposing position**]; we will do better on our yearly tests [**2nd opposing position**]; and we are developing responsibility, good study habits, and time management skills [**3rd opposing position**].

While I agree that some homework is needed [**phrase used to introduce arguments**], there are other factors teachers should consider. First [**transition word**], practice does make perfect, but too much practice becomes tedious [**1st argument**]. If students are constantly battling homework, how motivated will they be to do well on their yearly tests [**2nd argument**]? Homework is supposed to develop responsibility, good study habits, and time management skills. For most kids, nearly everything they do from cleaning their room to yard work is to help them develop responsibility [**illustration**]. Secondly [**transition word**], do students have to do homework every single night to learn good study habits and manage their time? Wouldn't a couple nights a week do the trick [**further explanation**]? Finally [**transition word**], excessive homework might force some not to participate in after-school activities, not to get enough outdoor exercise, and cut into their family time [**further argument**].

A more sensible approach to homework can be reached [**restatement of issue**]. With limited homework, kids can still work to retain the skills learned in school [**reiteration of position**]. They will still be prepared to do well on their yearly texts. Finally, they will still be responsible with good study habits [**restatement of argument**], while having time to spend with their families and participating in healthy activities [**summarizing with an emotional appeal**].

## Annotated Mentor Text: Formal Persuasive Essay

Demonstrating topic, issue, topic sentence, position statement, position sentence stem, opposing positions, arguments, illustrations, transition words, and summarizing

# A Mathematician Comes to Know an Orange

The mentor text below is annotated to support you during instruction. The student version of this text is provided on the Digital Resource CD (mentortext6.pdf).

It sits balanced on my desk, radiant in its orange, setting-sun-glow **[sensory detail: sight]**. I know that even a slight prod with my finger would send it rolling like a ball away from me over the side of my desk to the floor. From my qualitative view, it is round like the moon **[sensory detail: sight]** and with a pitted, rubbery **[sensory detail: touch]** skin. Cool to the touch **[sensory detail: touch]** and about the size of a baseball, it fits comfortably in my hand. I lift it to my nose and can almost smell the citrus zest **[sensory detail: smell]** held captive beneath its peel. I call it by its name, *Navel*. Named as such because at its apex it appears to have what looks like a human belly-button **[sensory detail: sight]**.

With my quantitative lens, I record: Weight—25 grams; diameter—8 mm; circumference—2.5 cm; radius—4 mm; and skin thickness 1.5 mm. I count 11 sections. Slowly, I bite into Navel. Its seedless pulp has a sweet, satisfying sensation **[sensory Detail: taste]**. As juice runs down my chin, I am instantly whisked away to carefree summer days drenched in sunlight **[sensory detail: taste and feeling]**

My orange and I have become one.

### Annotated Mentor Text: Descriptive

Demonstrating Sensory Details (sight, sound, taste, touch, and feeling)

# Ratio

The mentor text below is annotated to support you during instruction. The student version of this text is provided on the Digital Resource CD (mentortext7.pdf).

A ratio is a comparison or relation between the quantities of two different things [**topic and topic sentence**]. For example [**transition word**], take our math class [**detail: illustration**]. There are 35 students: 15 girls and 20 boys [**information**]. The ratio of girls to boys would be set up first as 15 to 20 [**detail: fact**]. When expressing the ratio in words, we use the word <u>to</u> between the two numbers [**detail: further explanation**]. However [**transition word**], we would need to simplify the ratio by asking ourselves, *What one number is each quantity divisibleby with the answer being a whole number with no remainder?* This is called the *divisibility rule* and in this case, both the 15 and the 20 can be divided equally by 5. So 15 divided by 5 equals 3, and 20 divided by 5 equals 4. We can now say that the ratio of girls to boys in our math class is 3 to 4 [**detail: further explanation**]. It is important to remember when writing ratios that the order of the quantities, or numbers, is critical [**detail: fact**. Since we were comparing girls to boys and not boys to girls, we would need to put the simplified representing the girls (3) first in the expression and the simplified number representing the boys (4) second. To be correct then, we would say 3 to 4, not 4 to 3 [**detail: further explanation**]. We could, also, write it as 3:4. Here we simply use a colon (:) instead of *to* between the two numbers [**detail: fact**].

Another way to express a ratio is to present it as a fraction. In the case of the girls and boys in my math class, it would be $\frac{15}{20}$ or fifteen twentieths [**detail: fact**]. When presenting a ratio as a fraction, the first quantity (15) is the numerator (top number) and the second quantity becomes the denominator (bottom number) [**detail: fact**]. Also [**transition word**], when expressing a ratio as a fraction, we need to reduce the fraction to its lowest common denominator. Here again we apply the "divisibility rule". See that $\frac{15}{20}$ can be reduced to the fraction $\frac{3}{4}$ [**detail: further explanation**]. Now all three ways to present the ratio of girls to boys tell us one thing: There are 3 girls for every 4 boys in our math class [**detail: illustration**].

\* content-specific words are underlined

## Annotated Mentor Text: Informational/Explanatory

Demonstrating topic, topic sentence, information, details (facts, illustrations, and further explanations or reasons), transition words, and content-specific words.

Name: _____ Date: _____

# Soccer Paragraph Frame 1

**Directions:** Use the paragraph frame to explain how you solved the problem.

A soccer team stopped at a restaurant after a game. They divided into two groups. One group bought 5 ham sandwiches and 7 slices of pizza for a cost of $24.90. The second group spent $28.80 and bought 5 ham sandwiches and 9 slices of pizza. How much does a slice of pizza cost?

In order to find out how much each slice of pizza cost, I had to use two steps.

I first _____

_____

_____ .

After that, I _____

_____ .

Therefore, I know _____

_____ .

Name: _____ Date:_____

# Novels Paragraph Frame 1

**Directions:** Use the paragraph frame to explain how you solved the problem.

A school ordered 157 novels this year. This is 13 more than twice the number of novels that were ordered last year. How many novels were ordered last year?

In order to find out how many novels were ordered, I had to use two steps.

I first _____

_____

_____ .

After that, I _____

_____ .

Therefore, I know _____

_____

_____ .

Name: _____ Date:_____

# Bowling Paragraph Frame 1

**Directions:** Use the paragraph frame to explain how you solved the problem.

> Oscar scored fewer 50 points fewer in his second bowling game than in his first game. His total score for two games was 376. How many points did he score in each game?

In order to find out how many points Oscar scored in each bowling game, I had to use two steps.

I first _____

_____

_____ .

After that, I _____

_____ .

Therefore, I know _____

_____

_____ .

Name: _____ Date: _____

# Zoo Tickets Paragraph Frame 1

**Directions:** Use the paragraph frame to explain how you solved the problem.

> At the local zoo, a student admission ticket costs $2.50 and an adult admission ticket costs $4.50. If 152 student tickets were sold, and the total sales were $587, how many adult tickets were sold?

In order to find out how many adult tickets were sold, I had to use three steps.

To solve the problem, I first _____

_____

_____ .

After that, I _____

_____

_____ .

Next, _____

_____ .

Therefore, I know _____

_____

_____ .

Name: _____ Date:_____

# Tips Paragraph Frame 1

**Directions:** Use the paragraph frame to explain how you solved the problem.

> Jackie worked at the All You Can Eat Restaurant for an hourly wage plus tips. She was paid $5.25 per hour. She worked a total of 48 hours at the restaurant, and by the end of the summer she had earned—between both her wages and her tips—a total of $564.00. On an average, how much was she making in tips per hour?

In order to find out how much Jackie earned in tips per hour, I used three steps.

To solve the problem, I first _____

_____

_____ .

After that, I _____

_____

_____

Next, _____

_____ .

Therefore, I know _____

_____

_____ .

Name: _____  Date: _____

# Tires Paragraph Frame 1

**Directions:** Use the paragraph frame to explain how you solved the problem.

> Javier works at his grandfather's store selling tires. His grandfather pays him $100 per week plus $2.25 per tire sold. How many tires would have to be sold for Javier to earn between $130 and $140 next week?

In order to find out how may tires Javier would have to sell to earn between $130 and $140 next week, I used three steps.

To solve the problem, I first _____

_____

_____ .

After that, I _____

_____

_____

Next, _____

_____ .

Therefore, I know _____

_____

_____ .

Name: _____  Date: _____

# Explaining Your Math Thinking in Words

## How did you do?

## Rubric Criteria

Students' problem-solving explanation will be scored as follows:

| | | Score |
|---|---|---|
| **Labels** | • **1 Point**: Limited labels are used in the explanation.<br>• **2 Points**: Correct labels are used throughout the explanation. | |
| **Math Vocabulary** | • **1 Point**: Limited math vocabulary is used in the explanation.<br>• **2 Points**: Some math vocabulary is used but incorrectly in math sentences.<br>• **3 Points**: Math vocabulary is used and correctly written in math sentences. | |
| **Problem-Solving Process Explanation** | • **1 Point**: The steps in the problem-solving process are incomplete or not explained; limited or no transition/sequence words are used.<br><br>• **2 Points**: The steps ("what") in the problem-solving process are presented but the mathematical reasoning ("why") behind each step is not; transition/sequence words are used but "why" words are not.<br><br>• **3 Points**: The steps ("what") in the problem-solving process are presented but not all the mathematical reasoning ("why") behind each step is presented; transition/sequence and "why" words are used but not in a logical way.<br><br>• **4 Points**: The steps ("what") in the problem-solving process are presented, each with the mathematical reasoning ("why") behind the steps; transition/sequence and "why" words are used correctly, but the overall explanation does not read smoothly.<br><br>• **5 Points**: The steps ("what") in the problem-solving process are presented, each with the mathematical reasoning ("why") behind the steps; transition/sequence and "why" words are used correctly and logically; the overall explanation is clear and reads smoothly. | |

Explained the steps of the process in a way that is both logical (explained the "what" and "why" of your steps) and readable (used transition words).

## Did you hit the 10?

## Your Total Score:

# Addressing Word Problems

## Read → Decide → Estimate → Work → Explain

**1.** **Read the Problem**

- What is happening in the problem?
- What do I know?
- What don't I know?
- What is the problem asking me to find out?

**2.** **Decide**

- What operation(s) will I need to do to solve the problem?
- What strategy will I use to solve the problem?

**3.** **Make an Estimation**

What is a reasonable answer?

**4.** **Work the Problem**

Check my work.

**5.** **Explain My Math Thinking in Writing**

# Farmer Arturo's Cows Sample

1. Farmer Arturo's Cows in the pasture

MOO MOO MOO MOO MOO

Key

= 10 cows

**MOO** = 1 cow

2. After his gate is left opened

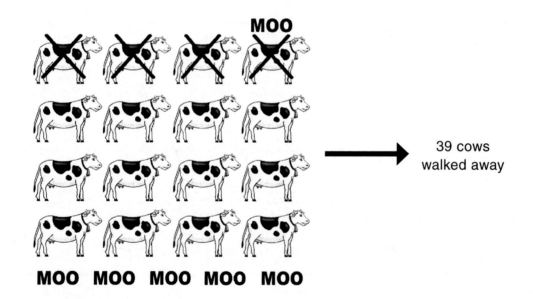

39 cows
walked away

MOO MOO MOO MOO MOO

3. 
$$
\begin{array}{r}
165 \\
-\ 39 \\
\hline
\end{array}
$$

 #51051—*Think It, Show It Mathematics*

Name: _____ Date:_____

# One-Step Problems

**Directions:** Complete the steps below to write a framed paragraph.

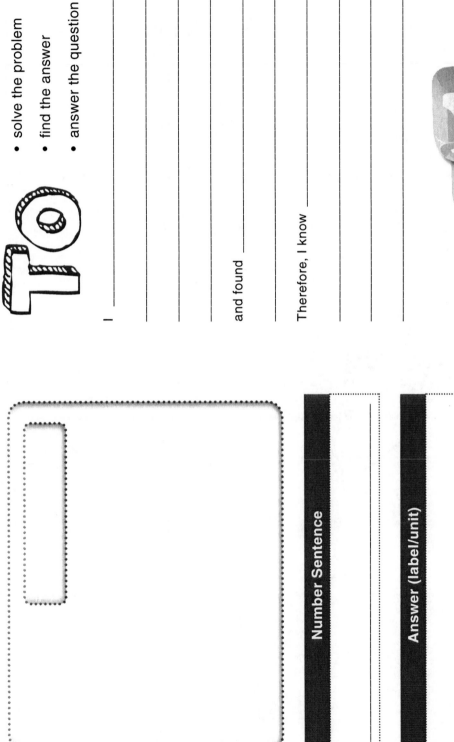

• solve the problem
• find the answer
• answer the question

_____

_____

_____

and found _____

_____

Therefore, I know _____

_____

**Number Sentence** _____

**Answer (label/unit)** _____

# Math Symbols and Math Words

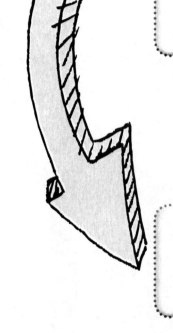

+ Addition

− Subtraction

= Equals

x Multiplication

÷ Division

165 − 39 = 126

# Math Symbols and Math Words *(cont.)*

**Number Sentences Use Math Symbols**

**Written Sentences Use Math Words**

| | | |
|---|---|---|
| + Addition |  | plus, added, combined |
| − Subtraction |  | minus, subtracted from, take away |
| = Equals |  | equaled |
| × Multiplication |  | multiply, product, times |
| ÷ Division | | divide, quotient |

Name: _____ Date:_____

# Break It Down

**Directions:** Complete the graphic organizer below to write a number sentence.

Find the Answer

Write as a Number Sentence

Remember that Number Sentences
use Math Symbols

$+ \; - \; \times \; \div$

Write as a Written Sentence

Remember that written sentences
use math words.

*add, plus, combined, subtracted, take away, divided by,
multiplied by, times, equals*

Name: _____ Date: _____

# Two-Step Problems

**Directions:** Complete the steps below to write a framed paragraph.

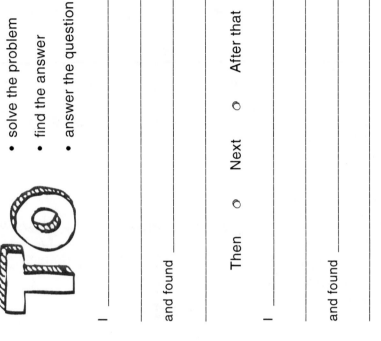

- solve the problem
- find the answer
- answer the question

I _____

and found _____

Then ◌ _____ Next ◌ _____ After that

I _____

and found _____

Therefore, I know _____

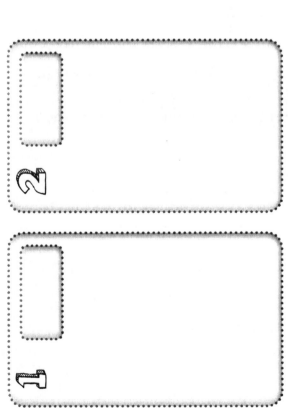

**1** 

**2** 

**Number Sentence**

1 _____

2 _____

**Answer (label/unit)**

_____

Name: _____  Date: _____

# Explain and Gain the Concept

**Directions:** Complete the graphic organizer below to explain your mathematical thinking.

 **Step 1**

What is happening in the problem? • What do I know? • What is my data? • What don't I know? • What is the problem asking me to find out?

| Data: Number Facts | What will my answer tell me? |
|---|---|
|  |  |

**Step 2**

Using my data, what mathematical operation(s) will I need to do to solve the problem?

 **Step 3**

Work the problem.  Check your work.

**Step 4**

Explain your math thinking.  How did you solve the problem?

_____

_____

_____

_____

_____

_____

_____

_____

# Explaining Your Math Thinking in Writing

✓ **Use math vocabulary** in correct math sentences

✓ Include all your **data: Number Facts**

✓ Use **transition words**

✓ **Explain** the why of your steps

✓ **Write** in complete sentences

✓ **Label** your answer

✓ **Proofread** your writing

### Words to help explain the why of your steps

- Since
- Because
- Therefore, I am

### Transition Words

- To start with
- First
- Then
- Next
- After that
- Second
- Finally

### Remember...

Always read your answer quietly to yourself.

Name: _____ Date:_____

# Comparisons and Contrasts

**Directions:** Fill in the blanks below to describe the similarities and differences between your two chosen objects or concepts.

| **Topic:** |
|---|

| **Subjects:**                              and |
|---|

| **Comparisons:** (Similarities) |
|---|

**1.** _____

_____

**2.** _____

_____

**3.** _____

_____

**4.** _____

_____

| **Contrasts:** (Differences) |
|---|

**1.** _____

_____

**2.** _____

_____

**3.** _____

_____

**4.** _____

_____

# Math Concept Files

**Card 1:** word or concept

**Card 2:** definition

**Card 3:** used in a mathematically correct way

**Card 4:** a real-life example is given

**Card 5:** a simple word problem is created using the word or concept

**Card 6:** listing of other related words and/or concepts

Name: _____ Date: _____

# What/Why Justification Sheet

**Directions:** Complete the graphic organizer to explain your thinking while solving a problem.

| Tell **what** steps you did to solve the problem. | Explain **why** you did the steps that you did. |
| --- | --- |
| | |

**Transition Words:**
- to start with
- then
- next
- after that
- first
- second
- third
- finally

**Why Words:**
- since
- because
- therefore, I know

Name: _____ Date:_____

# Thinking and Justifying

**Directions:** Complete the graphic organizer to explain your problem-solving process.

 **Step 1** What is happening in the problem? • What do I know? • What is my data? • What don't I know? • What is the problem asking me to find out?

| Data: Number Facts | What will my answer tell me? |
|---|---|
| | |

Tell what steps you will need to do to solve the problem.

 **Step 2**

Tell why you need to do these steps to solve the problem.

| **Transition words:** | • to start with  • then | • next  • after that | • first  • second | • third  • finally |
|---|---|---|---|---|

| **Why words:** | • since  • because | • therefore, I know | | |

Name: _____ Date:_____

# How Did They Do?
# Peer Scoring Rubric

**Directions:** Solve the problem in the work area. Then, fill in the rubric below to evaluate a classmate.

### Work Area

|  | Student 1 | Student 2 | Student 3 | Student 4 | Student 5 |
|---|---|---|---|---|---|
| **1 or 2 Points** <br> Used correct labels throughout their answer |  |  |  |  |  |
| **1, 2, or 3 Points** <br> Used math vocabulary in correct math sentences. |  |  |  |  |  |
| **1, 2, 3, 4, or 5 Points** <br> Explained the steps of the process in a way that is both logical and readable. |  |  |  |  |  |
| **Total** |  |  |  |  |  |

Name: _____ Date: _____

# Thinking through Your Writing

**Directions:** Fill in the blanks below to record ideas and questions on your chosen topic.

**Topic** _____

_____

**Purpose** _____

_____

_____

**Information Questions**

1. _____

_____

2. _____

_____

3. _____

_____

4. _____

_____

**Form** _____

Name: _____ Date:_____

# Add-an-Attribute Planning Sheet

**Directions:** Use the questions below to guide your research.  Record the answers to the questions in the space provided.

| My Shape | |
|---|---|

- How many sides does it have?
- How many angles does it have?
- How many sides are equal length?
- Does it have parallel sides?
- Are any of the angles congruent?
- What are the sides of the shape called?
- Other interesting facts

Name: _____ Date: _____

# Add-an-Attribute Planning Sheet

**Directions:** Choose a topic and write it in the space below. Record questions you want to answer about your topic. Write the answers to the questions in the space provided.

| My Number | **Questions to Consider** |
| --- | --- |
| | • How many digits does the number have? |
| | • Is the number even or odd? |
| | • What is the range of the number? |
| | • Can the number be factored, or is it prime? |
| | • Other interesting facts |

Name: _____ Date:_____

# Add-an-Attribute Planning Sheet

**Directions:** Choose a topic and write it in the space below. Record questions you want to answer about your topic. Write the answers to the questions in the space provided.

**My Topic**

**Questions to Consider**

- 
- 
- 
- 
- 
- 
- Other interesting facts

Name: _____ Date:_____

# Plot Diagram

**Directions:** Complete the plot diagram to begin the first step of your narrative.

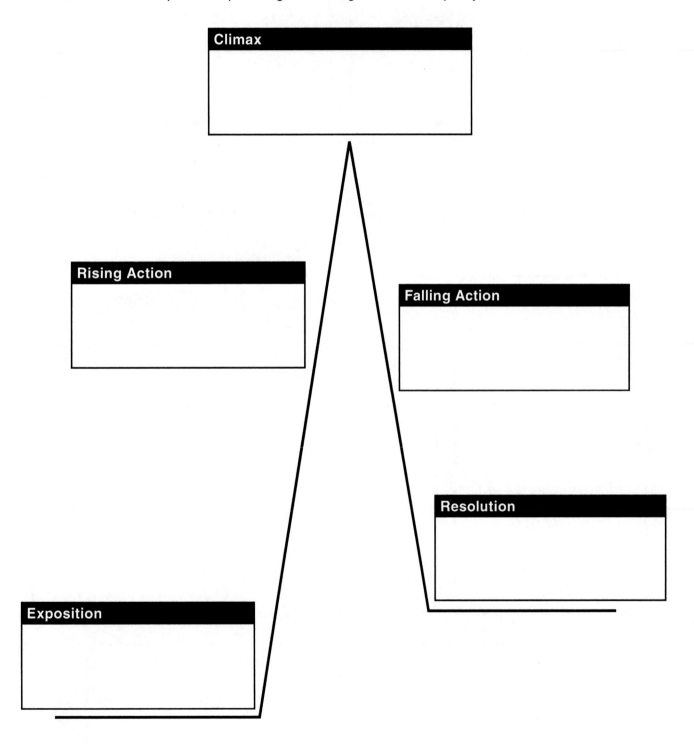

Name: _____ Date:_____

# Story Map

| Characters | Setting |
|---|---|
|  |  |

**Problem**

## Story Events

| Beginning | Middle | End |
|---|---|---|
|  |  |  |

**Resolution**

# Opinion, Reason, and Restated Opinion

**1. Topic Question**

Begin with a topic question to focus your writing.

**2. Opinion Sentence**

Write an opening sentence clearly stating your opinion (what you think). Use one of these sentence stems to start your sentence: *I think, I don't think, I believe, I don't believe, In my opinion.*

**3. Reason Sentences**

Continue by writing two or more sentences with the different reasons you have for your opinion (why you think what you think). Use one of our transition words with each sentence: *first, second, also, next, finally, in addition, besides.*

**4. Restated Opinion Sentence**

Finish by writing a sentence in which you restate your opinion (what you think) but try to say it in different words.

Name: _____ Date:_____

# Opposing Reasons/Your Argument Planning Sheet

**Directions:** Complete the activity sheet to record opposing reasons and your argument against those reasons.

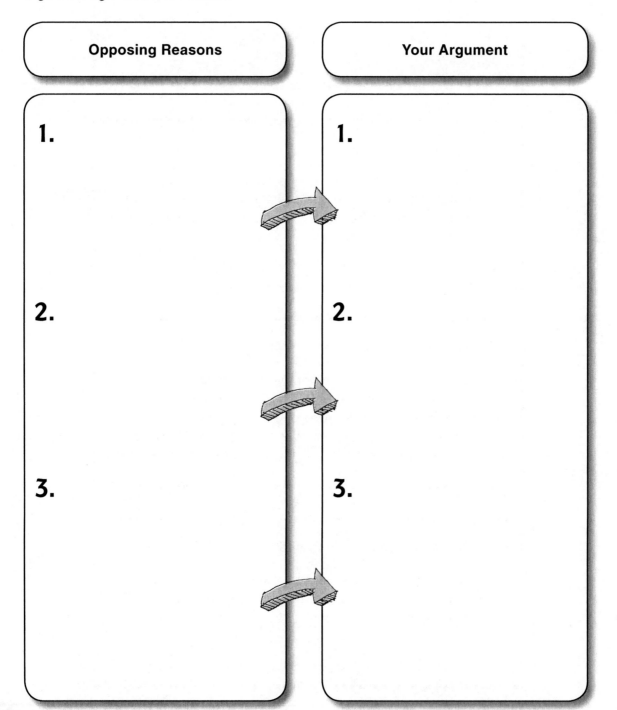

| **Opposing Reasons** | **Your Argument** |
|---|---|
| 1. | 1. |
| 2. | 2. |
| 3. | 3. |

# How to Structure a Persuasive Essay

**Begin** (Introduction):

- Engaging topic sentence(s)
- Explanation of the issue
- Clearly stated writer's position on the issue

- Helpful words and phrases:
  - in my opinion
  - I believe
  - it is my belief that
  - from my point of view
  - I question whether
  - I (dis)agree
  - I maintain that
  - there is no doubt that

**Continue** (Body of the essay):

- Mathematical reasons or arguments to support writer's position while addressing possible opposing positions
- Examples, logic, and/or mathematical evidence to support each point

- Helpful words and phrases:
  - first
  - to begin with
  - next
  - because
  - since
  - for example
  - finally
  - last
  - consequently
  - in addition
  - according to
  - I believe
  - in my opinion
  - in my experience
  - although
  - despite
  - on the other hand
  - still
  - moreover
  - besides
  - similarly
  - further
  - for example
  - in fact
  - as evidence
  - for instance
  - in support of this
  - I personally believe

**Finish** (Conclusion):

- Restatement of the issue and the writer's position (try not to use the exact wording you used in your Introduction)
- Reiteration of key or most powerful points of writer's reasons and arguments (again trying not to use the same wording used in the body of your essay)
- Ending with a strong summarizing statement(s)...possibly making a powerful personal or emotional appeal

- Helpful words and phrases:
  - to sum up
  - in short
  - in brief
  - as you can see
  - as I have explained
  - in summation
  - in other words
  - in conclusion
  - in any event
  - as I have noted
  - obviously
  - as you can see
  - without a doubt

Name: _____ Date: _____

# Topic, Issue, and Position Statement Planning Grid

**Directions:** Complete the questions below to outline your argument.

**Topic:** _____

_____

**Issue:** _____

_____

**Position Statement:** _____

_____

**Background Information:** _____

_____

**Reasons that Support My Position:**

**1.** _____

_____

_____

**2.** _____

_____

_____

**3.** _____

_____

# Persuasive/Argument Words

**Topic Sentence Phrases:**

- in my opinion
- I believe
- it is my belief that
- I question whether
- I (dis)agree

**Presenting Information Words and Phrases:**

- first
- second
- third
- finally
- last
- one way
- a second way
- another way (method, means, technique, approach, tactic)
- furthermore
- also
- in addition
- besides
- next
- moreover

**Phrases to Introduce Reasoning and Evidence:**

- for example
- in fact
- for a case in point
- as evidence
- for instance
- in support of this

**Cause and Effect Words and Phrases:**

- since
- because
- due to
- for this reason
- therefore
- caused by
- as a result of
- consequently
- leads to
- is responsible for
- in effect
- brought about
- made possible

Name: _____ Date: _____

# Descriptive Writing Planning Sheet

**Directions:** Write your topic in the center. Add details that match the description in each additional box.

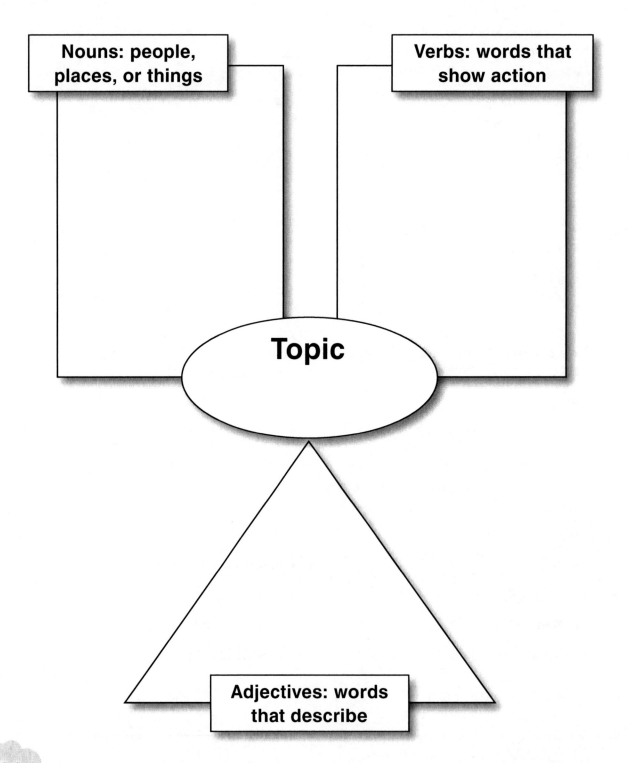

**Nouns: people, places, or things**

**Verbs: words that show action**

**Topic**

**Adjectives: words that describe**

Name: _____ Date: _____

# Descriptive Writing Brainstorming Guide

**Directions:** Write your topic in the space below. Brainstorm ideas in the available space. Use all your senses.

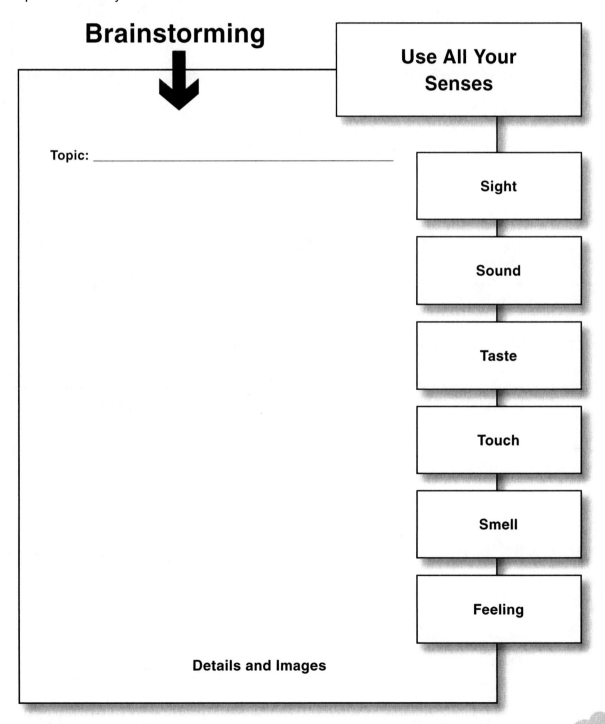

**Brainstorming**

**Use All Your Senses**

Topic: _____

Sight

Sound

Taste

Touch

Smell

Feeling

**Details and Images**

Name: _____ Date: _____

# Explanatory Text Planning Web

**Directions:** Write your topic in the center space. Add details and additional information in the appropriate spaces below.

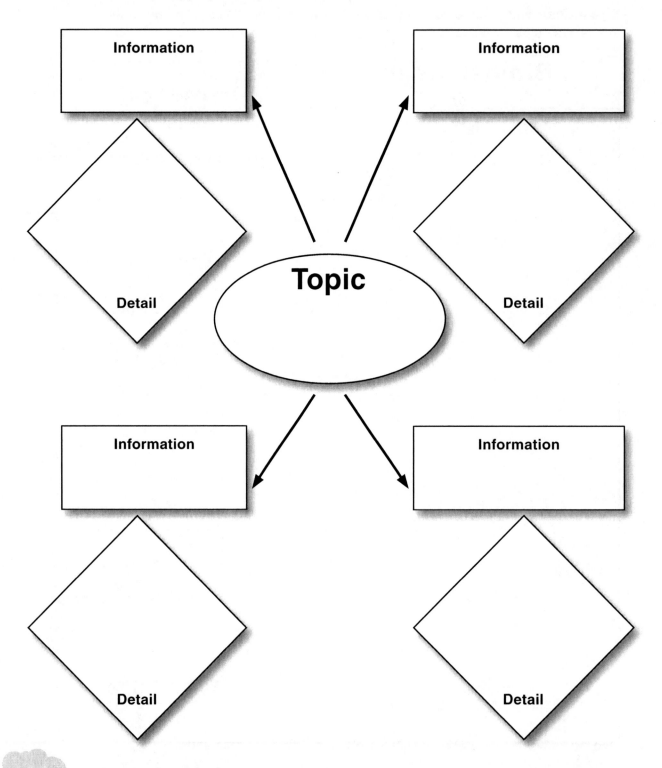

Name: _____ Date: _____

# Explanatory Text Planning Chart

**Directions:** Write your topic at the top of the activity sheet. Add details and additional information in the appropriate spaces below.

**Topic**

**Information**

**Information**

**Details**

**Details**

Name: _____ Date: _____

# Procedural Texts

**Directions:** Write your topic on the first line.  Complete the rest of the activity sheet according to the guidelines provided.

**Topic:** _____

**Introductory Sentence:** _____

_____

_____

_____

**Steps:** _____

_____

_____

_____

_____

_____

_____

_____

_____

_____

_____

**Transition Words:** first, then, after that, so now, finally, next

# Writing in Math

## Writing in Math

**Mathematical Vocabulary and Language**

**Writing Purposes and Types**

**Writing to:**

- explain
- define
- persuade
- describe
- justify
- show procedure

**Writing types:**

- persuasive
- exp/inf
- descriptive
- compare/contrast
- narrative
- procedural

**Mathematical Skills, Concepts and Principles**

The "how", "what", and "why" of mathematics

Name: _____ Date: _____

# Writing Data Analysis Statements

**Directions:** Fill in the blanks and circle the words to complete the activity sheet.

The     bar graph

         data table     shows

         line graph     tells me

         circle graph     demonstrates     that

_____

_____.

(Data interpretation: What I know)

I know because _____

_____.

         But

         While

         Whereas

         In contrast to_____

_____.

(Evidence statement: How I know it.)

Additional evidence statements can begin with transition words such as *also* or *another way*.

Name: _____ Date: _____

# Writing a Scientific Conclusion

**Directions:** Fill in the blanks and circle the words to write your scientific conclusion.

**Investigation Question**

_____

_____

_____ .

**Answer Statement**

_____

_____

_____ .

Use key words from the Investigation Question and turn it into a
statement that directly answers the question.

**Evidence Statement**

I

We know this because _____

_____ .

(data)

But

While

Whereas

In contrast to _____

_____ .

(contrasting data)

Additional evidence statements can begin with transition words such as
*also* or *another way.*

# Writing a Scientific Conclusion *(cont.)*

**Hypothesis Statement**

This    data      refutes    my

      evidence    confirms    our    hypothesis because _____

_____

_____

_____ .

**Inference Statement**

I

We    think the outcome of    my      investigation      was a result of

                                our          was caused by

                                                happened because

_____

_____

_____

_____ .

# Writing a Scientific Conclusion *(cont.)*

**Conclusion Statement**

Therefore

In conclusion,    I

             we    now know &#95;&#95;&#95;&#95;&#95;&#95;&#95;&#95;&#95;&#95;&#95;&#95;&#95;&#95;&#95;&#95;

&#95;&#95;&#95;&#95;&#95;&#95;&#95;&#95;&#95;&#95;&#95;&#95;&#95;&#95;&#95;&#95;&#95;&#95;&#95;&#95;&#95;&#95;&#95;&#95;

&#95;&#95;&#95;&#95;&#95;&#95;&#95;&#95;&#95;&#95;&#95;&#95;&#95;&#95;&#95;&#95;&#95;&#95;&#95;&#95;&#95;&#95;&#95; .

(A statement of what you have learned or now know as a result of the investigation)

**Real-life Statement**

&#95;&#95;&#95;&#95;&#95;&#95;&#95;&#95;&#95;&#95;&#95;&#95;&#95;&#95;&#95;&#95;&#95;&#95;&#95;&#95;&#95;&#95;&#95;&#95;

&#95;&#95;&#95;&#95;&#95;&#95;&#95;&#95;&#95;&#95;&#95;&#95;&#95;&#95;&#95;&#95;&#95;&#95;&#95;&#95;&#95;&#95;&#95;&#95;

&#95;&#95;&#95;&#95;&#95;&#95;&#95;&#95;&#95;&#95;&#95;&#95;&#95;&#95;&#95;&#95;&#95;&#95;&#95;&#95;&#95;&#95;&#95; .

(A statement of what real-life applications can be made as a result of what you learned)

**Further Investigations Statement**

&#95;&#95;&#95;&#95;&#95;&#95;&#95;&#95;&#95;&#95;&#95;&#95;&#95;&#95;&#95;&#95;&#95;&#95;&#95;&#95;&#95;&#95;&#95;&#95;

&#95;&#95;&#95;&#95;&#95;&#95;&#95;&#95;&#95;&#95;&#95;&#95;&#95;&#95;&#95;&#95;&#95;&#95;&#95;&#95;&#95;&#95;&#95;&#95;

&#95;&#95;&#95;&#95;&#95;&#95;&#95;&#95;&#95;&#95;&#95;&#95;&#95;&#95;&#95;&#95;&#95;&#95;&#95;&#95;&#95;&#95;&#95; .

(A statement of what further investigations might be conducted or what questions might be answered as a result of what you learned.)

# Comparative Writing Rubric

Name: _____     Date: _____

## Comparative Writing Rubric

**Math Content:** Is it complete, accurate, and contains no misconceptions?

| | 0 | 5 | 10 |
|---|---|---|---|
| **Content, Overall Clarity and Organization, and Content-Specific Vocabulary** <br><br> **Points:** | The reader has little or no chance of understanding the similarities and differences between its subjects. <br> • no topic sentence is included <br> • confusing organization <br> • important information and relevant details are lacking <br> • ineffective use, or no use, of transition words <br> • no use of topic's content-specific vocabulary | The reader may have some difficulty understanding exactly the similarities and differences between its subjects. <br> • topic statement not evident (or not clear enough) <br> • weak organization <br> • some information and/or details are provided, but not sufficiently <br> • transition words could have been chose more carefully <br> • limited use of topic's content-specific vocabulary | The paragraph(s) is written so the reader can easily understand the similarities and differences between its subjects. <br> • a clear and concise topic statement(s) is used <br> • well organized <br> • includes enough information and details to cover the topic <br> • transition words are effectively used <br> • content-specific vocabulary is utilized |
| **Style: Voice, Word Choice, and Sentence Fluency** <br><br> **Points:** | Writing is readable but with no sense that the author cared about his or her topic. <br> • sentences ramble and are repetitous <br> • careful word choices are not evident <br> • not interesting to listen to <br> • doesn't read well aloud | Writing includes: <br> • somewhat rambling and/or repetitious sentences <br> • limited use of accurate and precise word choices <br> • limited examples of figurative language (if appropriate) <br> • weak sentence structure variety | Writing includes: <br> • accurate and precise word choices <br> • example of figurative language (if appropriate) <br> • a variety of different sentence structures <br> • reads well aloud and is interesting to listen to |
| **Language Conventions: Mechanics and Grammar** <br><br> **Points:** | Language skills impede meaning. The writing is error-ridden. | Attempts to use: <br> • complete sentences in which the subject and verb agree appropriate) <br> • correct use of modifiers <br> • correct use of commas, apostrophes, and quotation marks <br> • abbreviations and capitals are used appropriately <br> • words are spelled correctly <br> • paragraphing aids readability | Writing has few errors that impede meaning. |

**Total Score:**

# Narrative Writing Rubric

Name: _____    Date: _____

## Narrative Writing Rubric

**Math Content:** Is it complete, accurate, and contains no misconceptions?

| | 0 | 5 | 10 |
|---|---|---|---|
| **Content, Overall Clarity and Organization, and Content-Specific Vocabulary**<br><br>Points: | The reader has little or no chance of understanding the *who, what and where* of this story.<br><br>• characters are not introduced and developed<br>• setting is not described<br>• details of the events in the story are not included<br>• no clear sequencing of the events or actions in the story (beginning, middle, and end)<br>• no use of content-specific vocabulary | The reader may have some difficulty thoroughly understanding the *who, what, and where* of the story<br><br>• characters appear in the story but are not fully developed<br>• limited description of setting<br>• events in the story could have been better elaborated<br>• sequencing of the story events and actions are sometimes confusing<br>• there is limited use of content-specific vocabulary | The story is written so the reader could easily understand and follow the story, its setting, and characters.<br><br>• characters are included, described, and developed<br>• setting is described in detail<br>• events are explained and elaborated<br>• the sequencing of events and actions are logical<br>• content-specific vocabulary is utilized |
| **Style: Voice, Word Choice, and Sentence Fluency**<br><br>Points: | Writing is readable but with no sense that the author cared about his or her topic.<br><br>• sentences ramble and are repetitous<br>• careful word choices are not evident<br>• not interesting to listen to<br>• doesn't read well aloud | Writing includes:<br><br>• somewhat rambling and/or repetitious sentences<br>• limited use of accurate and precise word choices<br>• limited examples of figurative language (if appropriate)<br>• weak sentence structure variety | Writing includes:<br><br>• example of figurative language (if appropriate)<br>• a variety of different sentence structures<br>• reads well aloud and is interesting to listen to |
| **Language Conventions: Mechanics and Grammar**<br><br>Points: | Language skills impede meaning. The writing is error-ridden. | Attempts to use:<br><br>• complete sentences in which the subject and verb agree appropriate)<br>• correct use of modifiers<br>• correct use of commas, apostrophes, and quotation marks<br>• abbreviations and capitals are used appropriately<br>• words are spelled correctly<br>• paragraphing aids readability | Writing has few errors that impede meaning. |

**Total Score:**

# Persuasive Writing Rubric

Name: _____ Date: _____

| Persuasive Writing Rubric | | | |
|---|---|---|---|
| | 0 | 5 | 10 |
| **Math Content:** Is it complete, accurate, and contains no misconceptions? | | | |
| **Content, Overall Clarity and Organization, and Content-Specific Vocabulary**<br><br>**Points:** | The reader has little or no chance of following and understanding the issue and arguments presented in this essay.<br>• no topic or position statement is presented<br>• arguments to opposing view are not logical and/or convincing<br>• ineffective use, or no use, of transition words.<br>• no summary statement is included<br>• no use of content-specific vocabulary | The reader may have some difficulty following and understanding the writer's position and arguments on the topic's issue.<br>• topic/position statements are not clear enough<br>• arguments are not as convincing as they could have been<br>• transition words could have been chosen more carefully<br>• summary is weak<br>• limited use of content-specific vocabulary | The essay is written so the reader can easily understand the writer's position and arguments.<br>• a clear topic/position statement is used<br>• arguments are logical and convincingly presented<br>• transition words are effectively used<br>• content-specific vocabulary is utilized<br>• powerful summary sentence is included |
| **Style: Voice, Word Choice, and Sentence Fluency**<br><br>**Points:** | Writing is readable but with no sense that the author cared about his or her topic.<br>• sentences ramble and are repetitous<br>• careful word choices are not evident<br>• not interesting to listen to<br>• doesn't read well aloud | Writing includes:<br>• somewhat rambling and/or repetitious sentences<br>• limited use of accurate and precise word choices<br>• limited examples of figurative language (if appropriate)<br>• weak sentence structure variety | Writing includes:<br>• accurate and precise word choices<br>• example of figurative language (if appropriate)<br>• a variety of different sentence structures<br>• reads well aloud and is interesting to listen to |
| **Language Conventions: Mechanics and Grammar**<br><br>**Points:** | Language skills impede meaning. The writing is error-ridden. | Attempts to use:<br>• complete sentences in which the subject and verb agree<br>• correct use of modifiers<br>• correct use of commas, apostrophes, and quotation marks<br>• abbreviations and capitals are used appropriately<br>• words are spelled correctly<br>• paragraphing aids readability | Writing has few errors that impede meaning. |
| **Total Score:** | | | |

Name: _____     Date: _____

# Descriptive Writing Rubric

## Descriptive Writing Rubric

**Math Content:** Is it complete, accurate, and contains no misconceptions?

| | 0 | 5 | 10 |
|---|---|---|---|
| **Content, Overall Clarity and Organization, and Content-Specific Vocabulary**<br><br>Points: | The reader has little or no chance of seeing "in their minds" what is being described in this essay.<br>• no topic sentence is evident<br>• confusing organization<br>• important information and relevant details are lacking<br>• little or no use of sensory words<br>• ineffective use, or no use, of transition words<br>• no use of topic's content-specific vocabulary | The reader may have some difficulty clearly picturing what is being described in this essay.<br>• topic sentence not clear enough<br>• weak organization<br>• some information and details are provided but not sufficiently<br>• limited use of sensory words and images<br>• transition words could have been chosen more effectively<br>• limited use of content-specific vocabulary | The essay is written so the reader can picture perfectly what was being described.<br>• a clear and consice topic statement is used<br>• includes enough information and details to cover topic<br>• used sensory words and images well<br>• transition words are effectivley used<br>• content-specific vocabulary is utilized |
| **Style: Voice, Word Choice, and Sentence Fluency**<br><br>Points: | Writing is readable but with no sense that the author cared about his or her topic.<br>• sentences ramble and are repetitous<br>• careful word choices are not evident<br>• not interesting to listen to<br>• doesn't read well aloud | Writing includes:<br>• somewhat rambling and/or repetitious sentences<br>• limited use of accurate and precise word choices<br>• limited examples of figurative language (if appropriate)<br>• weak sentence structure variety | Writing includes:<br>• accurate and precise word choices<br>• example of figurative language (if appropriate)<br>• a variety of different sentence structures<br>• reads well aloud and is interesting to listen to |
| **Language Conventions: Mechanics and Grammar**<br><br>Points: | Language skills impede meaning. The writing is error-ridden. | Attempts to use:<br>• complete sentences in which the subject and verb agree<br>• correct use of modifiers<br>• correct use of commas, apostrophes, and quotation marks<br>• abbreviations and capitals are used appropriately<br>• words are spelled correctly<br>• paragraphing aids readability | Writing has few errors that impede meaning. |
| **Total Score:** | | | |

# Informational/Explanatory Writing Rubric

Name: _____    Date: _____

## Informational/Explanatory Writing Rubric

| | 0 | 5 | 10 |
|---|---|---|---|
| **Math Content:** Is it complete, accurate, and contains no misconceptions? | | | |
| **Content, Overall Clarity and Organization, and Content-Specific Vocabulary**<br><br>**Points:** | The reader has little or no chance of learning about the topic written about in this essay.<br>• no clear topic sentence is included<br>• confusing organization<br>• important information is lacking<br>• few, if any, details or elaborations are included<br>• ineffective use (or no use) of transition words<br>• no use of topic's content-specific vocabulary | The reader may have some difficulty completely understanding what is being explained in this paragraph(s).<br>• topic statement not evident (or not clear enough)<br>• weak organization<br>• some information and details were given but not sufficiently<br>• transition words could have been chosen more effectively<br>• limited use of topic's content-specific vocabulary | The paragraph(s) is written so the reader could easily learn much about its topic.<br>• a clear topic statement(s) is used<br>• includes sufficient relevant information with supporting and elaborating details<br>• transition words are effectively used.<br>• content-specific vocabulary is utilized |
| **Style: Voice, Word Choice, and Sentence Fluency**<br><br>**Points:** | Writing is readable but with no sense that the author cared about his or her topic.<br>• sentences ramble and are repetitious<br>• careful word choices are not evident<br>• not interesting to listen to<br>• doesn't read well aloud | Writing includes:<br>• somewhat rambling and/or repetitious sentences<br>• limited use of accurate and precise word choices<br>• limited examples of figurative language (if appropriate)<br>• weak sentence structure variety | Writing includes:<br>• accurate and precise word choices<br>• example of figurative language (if appropriate)<br>• a variety of different sentence structures<br>• reads well aloud and is interesting to listen to |
| **Language Conventions: Mechanics and Grammar**<br><br>**Points:** | Language skills impede meaning. The writing is error-ridden. | Attempts to use:<br>• complete sentences in which the subject and verb agree<br>• correct use of modifiers<br>• correct use of commas, apostrophes, and quotation marks<br>• abbreviations and capitals are used appropriately<br>• words are spelled correctly<br>• paragraphing aids readability | Writing has few errors that impede meaning. |

**Total Score:** _____

# Student Exemplars (8th Grade)

**Quarter-Pound Hamburgers**

Stacy and Michelle were walking home from volleyball practice when they decided to have the whole team over that evening for homemade quarter-pound hamburgers. "Just like they have at the fast food restaurants," they said. When they got to Stacy's house, she looked in her refrigerator and saw that she had $5\frac{1}{2}$ pounds of ground beef. Then, the girls started to figure. They knew that there were 23 members on the team, including both of them, but that 2 were vegetarians and would not eat burgers. They also knew that $\frac{1}{7}$ of the members who are meat eaters would want 2 burgers. "Five and a half pounds will not be enough," Michelle said.

Is Michelle correct? Explain how you would calculate the amount of ground beef needed.

**Student Response 1**

To solve the problem, I had to first figure out how many total burgers the volleyball team would need. Since I knew that there were 23 members but that 2 were vegetarians and would not eat a burger, I subtracted 2 from the 23. This gave me 21. I then multiplied 21 by $\frac{1}{7}$ because $\frac{1}{7}$ of the team that would eat burgers would want 2 hamburgers. I found that they would need 3 additional burgers. Next, I added 21 and 3 and found that they would need to make a total of 24 burgers. Finally I multiplied the 24 by $\frac{1}{4}$ because they were quarter-pounders and found this equaled 6. Therefore I know—without a question—that Michelle was correct. Five and a half pounds would not be enough. They would need 6 pounds of ground beef to feed the entire team.

**Student Response 2**

Michelle is correct. The $5\frac{1}{2}$ pounds of ground beef would not be enough to feed the volleyball team quarter-pounders. To determine this, I first subtracted 23 minus 2 and found a difference of 21, so I knew that 21 girls would be eating. But since $\frac{1}{7}$ of them would eat two burgers, I needed to multiply $\frac{1}{7}$ times 21. When I did this, I found 3. This then told me that they would need 3 additional burgers. So I added the 3 burgers with the 21 burgers and found that the girls would need to make 24 burgers. And since they were making quarter-pounders, I divided the 24 by 4, giving me 6. Therefore, I know that Stacy and Michelle will need 6 pounds of ground beef if they want to feed the volleyball team.

# Student Exemplars (7th Grade)

**Tips and Wages**

Jackie worked at the All You Can Eat Restaurant for an hourly wage plus tips. She was paid $5.25 per hour. She worked a total of 48 hours at the restaurant and by the end of the summer had earned—between both her wages and her tips—a total of $564.00. On average, how much was she making in tips per hour? Explain how your found your answer.

**Student Response 1**

To start with, I multiplied $5.25 by 48 hours because I needed to figure out how much she made over the summer in wages alone. I found the answer to be $252.00. Next, I subtracted the $252.00 from the $564.00 because I needed to find out how much she made in tips over the summer. I found that answer to be $312.00. Since I needed to figure out how much she made in tips per hour, I then divided $312.00 by 48 to get $6.50. Therefore, I know she made $6.50 in tips per hour on average.

**Student Response 2**

First, I multiplied $5.25 by 48 hours because I wanted to know how much money she made from her hourly wages. After that, I subtracted her wages ($252.00) from her total earnings ($564.00) and found that she made $312.00 in tips. Finally, I divided her tip money by the hours that she had worked (48). Therefore, I know that Jackie made an average of $6.50 in tips per hour she worked.

# Student Exemplars (6th Grade)

**Running Ruben**

Running Ruben was a running fool,

Ran everyday to and from school.

If that wasn't enough for him to do,

He ran each and every Saturday too.

Yes, I say, Running Ruben was a running fool!

If Running Ruben's school is $2\frac{3}{4}$ miles from his house and his route on each Saturday is 7.2 miles, how many miles does he run in a week? Explain how you found your answer.

**Student Response 1**

Since Running Ruben's school is $2\frac{3}{4}$ miles away, I first needed to find out how far it was to school and back. I converted $2\frac{3}{4}$ to a decimal because I could do that it in my head. $2\frac{3}{4}$ is 2.75. So I added 2.75 and 2.75 and found a total of 5.50 miles. After that, I multiplied 5.50 miles times 5 because there are 5 school days in a week. This gave me 27.50 miles. Finally, I added the 7.2 miles that Ruben runs on Saturdays with the 27.50. Its sum was 34.7. Therefore, I know that crazy Running Ruben ran 34.7 miles each week.

**Student Response 2**

First off, I multiplied $2\frac{3}{4}$ times 2 because Running Ruben ran to and from school. I found $5\frac{1}{2}$ miles. Next, I multiplied the $5\frac{1}{2}$ times 5 because unless there was a holiday, Ruben ran 5 days Monday through Friday. This equaled $27\frac{1}{2}$ miles. But that fool boy also ran 7.2 miles on Saturday, so I had to add the 7.2 miles and the $27\frac{1}{2}$ miles. To do this, I had to convert $27\frac{1}{2}$ to a decimal. That made it 27.5. My last step was to add 27.5 and 7.2, giving a total of 34.7. Therefore, I know that Running Ruben ran 34.7 miles each and every week.

# Student Exemplars (5th Grade)

### Licorice

On her birthday, Shannon wants to give every fifth grader at her school one strand of licorice. There are six classes of fifth graders at her school, and each class has 30 students. Licorice comes in bags with 15 strands, and with tax, each bag will cost $1.19. How much money will Shannon need to do this? Explain how you found your answer.

### Student Response 1

To start with, I knew that Shannon wanted to give every fifth grader a strand of licorice. So I first needed to find out how many fifth graders there were. Since the problem said that there were six classes with 30 students in each, I multiplied 6 times 30 and got (just joking) and found 180. I then divided 15 pieces of licorice, which equaled a bag, into 180 and found 12. I now knew that Shannon would need 12 bags and each bag cost $1.19. So I multiplied 12 times $1.19 and found $14.28. Therefore, I know that Shannon will need to spend $14.28 to give everyone a piece of licorice.

### Student Response 2

Since Shannon was going to buy licorice for all the fifth graders, I multiplied 6 times 30 because there were 6 classes and each class had 30 students. I found 180. I then divided the 180 students by the 15 strands of licorice in a package. I did this to find out how many packages Shannon needs to buy. I found that she needs to buy 12 packages. Finally, I multiplied 12 times $1.19 because each package costs $1.19 and found $14.28. Therefore, I know Shannon needs to spend $14.28 to buy licorice for all the fifth graders.

# Student Exemplars (4th Grade)

### Buddy's Play Area

Ron and Susie want to have a penned-in area in their backyard so that Buddy, their dog, will have a grassy place in which to play. They bought 24 yards of fencing material to use for the fence and decided that the area will be a square. If they use the entire 24 yards of fence, how many square yards of grass will Buddy have to play in? Explain how you found your answer.

### Student Response 1

First I drew a square on the back of my paper because the problem said that Ron and Susie were going to build Buddy's play area in the shape of a square. Next, since I knew that a square has 4 equal sides and that they were going to use 24 yards of fencing material, I divided 4 into 24 in my head and wrote 6 yards for each side on my square. Finally, since I knew that length times width always equals the area, I multiplied 6 by 6 and found the product of 36. Therefore, I know that Buddy will have 36 square yards in his play area.

### Student Response 2

To start with, I had to divide 24 yards of fence by 4 because there are 4 equal sides on a square, and Ron and Susie were going to make a square pen. I found each side would be 6 yards. After doing that, I needed to find the square yardage of the fenced in area. To do this, I multiplied the length of the area by the width. I knew that 6 times 6 equals 36. Therefore, I know that Buddy will have 36 square yards where he can play and poop.

# Student Exemplars (3rd Grade)

### Picking Oranges with Bill and Frank

Bill and Frank decided to pick oranges at a farm one Saturday for some extra spending money. Bill worked very hard and filled three boxes while Frank goofed off most of the day and only filled one-half of a box. If each box holds 26 oranges, how many more oranges did Bill pick than Frank?

### Student Response 1

Since Bill filled three boxes of oranges and each box had 26 oranges, I multiplied 26 times 3 and found 78. So I knew that Bill had picked 78 oranges. But Frank was lazy and only picked $\frac{1}{2}$ of a box, so I thought that $\frac{1}{2}$ of 26 is 13. Then, all I had to do was subtract the 13 from 78. I found 65. Therefore, I know that Bill picked 65 more oranges than did Frank.

### Student Response 2

First, I multiplied 26 times 3 because each box held 26 oranges and Bill had picked 3 boxes. I found that the product was 78. And since Frank only picked $\frac{1}{2}$ of a box, I divided 26 by 2 because dividing a number by 2 gives you half of that number. I found an answer of 13. Finally, I subtracted 13 from 78 because Bill picked 78 oranges and Jim picked 13 oranges. I found that the answer is 65 oranges. Therefore, I know that Bill picked 65 more oranges than did that goof-off Frank.

# Recommended Literature

Adamson, Thomas Kristian. 2011. *Basketball: The Math of the Game*. North Mankato: Capstone Press.

Anno, Masaichiro, and Mitsumasa Anno. 1993. *Anno's Hat Tricks*. New York: Harcourt Publishing.

_____. 1999. *Anno's Magic Seeds*. New York: Puffin.

_____. 1999. *Anno's Mysterious Multiplying Jar*. New York: Penguin Putnam Books for Young Readers.

Barry, David. 1994. *The Rajah's Rice: A Mathematical Folktale from India*. Chicago: Children's Press Publishing.

Calvert, Pam. 2006. *Multiplying Menace: The Revenge of Rumpelstiltskin*. Watertown, MA: Charlesbridge.

Clemens, Meg, Sean Clemens, and Glenn Clemens. 2003. *The Everything Kids' Math Puzzles Book: Brain Teasers, Games, and Activities for Hours of Fun*. Avon, MA: Adams Media.

Demi. 1997. *One Grain of Rice: A Mathematical Folktale*. New York: Scholastic Press.

Ellis, Julie. 2010. *Pythagoras and the Ratios: A Math Adventure*. Watertown, MA: Charlesbridge.

Frederick, Shane Gerald. 2004. *What's Your Angle, Pythagoras? A Math Adventure*. Watertown, MA: Charlesbridge.

_____. 2011. *Football: The Math of the Game*. North Mankato, MN: Capstone Press.

Hoffman, Paul. 1998. *The Man Who Loved Numbers: The Story of Paul Erdos and the Search for Mathematical Truth*. New York: Hyperion.

Juster, Norton. 2000. *The Dot and the Line: A Romance in Lower Mathematics*. San Francisco: Chronicle Books.

Leedy, Loreen. 1996. *2 x 2 = Boo: A Set of Spooky Multiplication Stories*. New York: Holiday House.

Long, Lynette. 2000. *Dazzling Division: Games and Activities That Make Math Easy and Fun*. Somerset, NJ: Wiley.

Mills, Claudia. 2004. *7 x 9 = Trouble!*. New York: Farrar, Straus, and Giroux.

# Recommended Literature *(cont.)*

Mori, Tuyosi. 1986. *Socrates and the Three Little Pigs*. New York: Philomel.

Murphy, Stuart J. 1997. *Divide and Ride*. New York: HarperCollins.

Neuschwander, Cindy. 1997. *Sir Cumference and the First Round Table: A Math Adventure*. Watertown, MA: Charlesbridge Publishing.

_____. 1998. *Amanda Bean's Amazing Dream: A Mathematical Story*. New York: Scholastic Press.

_____. 2002. *Sir Cumference and the Dragon of Pi: A Math Adventure*. New York: Scholastic Press.

Pappas, Theoni. 1991. *Math Talk: Mathematical Ideas in Poems for Two Voices*. San Jose, CA: Wide World Publishing.

Pinczes, Elinor J. 2002. *A Remainder of One*. San Anselmo, CA: Sandpiper Press.

Poskitt, Kjartan. 1999. *Murderous Maths*. New York: Scholastic Press.

Reimer, Luetta, and Reimer, Wilbert. 1995. *Mathematicians Are People, Too: Stories from the Lives of Great Mathematicians*. Palo Alto, CA: Dale Seymour Publications.

Schechter, Bruce. 1998. *My Brain Is Open: The Mathematical Journeys of Paul Erdos*. New York: Simon & Schuster.

Schwartz, David M. 1994. *If You Made a Million*. New York: HarperCollins.

Scieszka, Jon. 1995. *Math Curse*. New York: Penguin Group.

_____. 2001. *Grapes of Math*. New York: Scholastic Press.

_____. 2002. *Math for All Seasons*. New York: Scholastic Press.

_____. 2003. *Math Appeal: Mind-Stretching Math Riddles*. New York: Scholastic Press.

_____. 2003. *Math-terpieces*. New York: Scholastic Press.

_____. 2004. *Math Fables*. New York: Scholastic Press.

_____. 2005. *Math Potatoes: Mind-stretching Brain Food*. New York: Scholastic Press.

_____. 2007. *Math Fables Too*. New York: Scholastic Press.

# Contents of the Digital Resource CD

| Page Number | Title | Filename |
|:---:|---|---|
| 134 | Soccer Paragraph Frame 1 | soccerframe1.pdf |
| 135 | Novels Paragraph Frame 1 | novelsframe1.pdf |
| 136 | Bowling Paragraph Frame 1 | bowlingframe1.pdf |
| 137 | Zoo Tickets Paragraph Frame 1 | zooticketsframe1.pdf |
| 138 | Tips Paragraph Frame 1 | tipsframe1.pdf |
| 139 | Tires Paragraph Frame 1 | tiresframe1.pdf |
| 140 | Explaining Your Math Thinking in Words | explaininwords.pdf |
| 141 | Addressing Word Problems | wordproblems.pdf |
| 142 | Farmer Arturo's Cows Sample | farmerarturo.pdf |
| 143 | One-Step Problems | onestepprob1.pdf<br>onestepprob2.pdf |
| 144–145 | Math Symbols and Math Words | symbolswords.pdf |
| 146 | Break It Down | breakitdown.pdf |
| 147 | Two-Step Problems | twostepprob1.pdf<br>twostepprob2.pdf |
| 148 | Explain and Gain the Concept | explaingain.pdf |
| 149 | Explaining Your Math Thinking in Writing | explaininwriting.pdf |
| 150 | Comparisons and Contrasts | compcontrast.pdf |
| 151 | Math Concept Files | mathconceptfiles.pdf |
| 152 | What/Why Justification Sheet | whatwhy.pdf |
| 153 | Thinking and Justifying | thinkjustify.pdf |
| 154 | How Did They Do?  Peer Scoring Rubric | scoringrubric.pdf |
| 155 | Thinking through Your Writing | thinkwriting.pdf |
| 156–158 | Add-an-Attribute Planning Sheet | attributesheet1.pdf<br>attributesheet2.pdf<br>attributesheet3.pdf |
| 159 | Plot Diagram | plotdiagram.pdf |
| 160 | Story Map | storymap.pdf |
| 161 | Opinion, Reason, and Restated Opinion | opinion.pdf |
| 162 | Opposing Reasons/Your Argument Planning Sheet | opposingreasons.pdf |

# Contents of the Digital Resource CD *(cont.)*

| Page Number | Title | Filename |
|---|---|---|
| 163 | How to Structure a Persuasive Essay | persuasiveessay.pdf |
| 164 | Topic, Issue, and Position Statement Planning Grid | topicissueposition.pdf |
| 165 | Persuasive/Argument Words | persuasivewords.pdf |
| 166 | Descriptive Writing Planning Sheet | descriptiveplan.pdf |
| 167 | Descriptive Writing Brainstorming Guide | desbrainstorming.pdf |
| 168 | Explanatory Text Planning Web | explanatoryweb.pdf |
| 169 | Explanatory Text Planning Chart | explanatorychart.pdf |
| 170 | Procedural Texts | proceduraltext.pdf |
| 171 | Writing in Math | writinginmath.pdf |
| 172 | Writing Data Analysis Statements | writingdata.pdf |
| 173–175 | Writing a Scientific Conclusion | scientificcon.pdf |
| 176 | Comparative Writing Rubric | compararubric.pdf |
| 177 | Narrative Writing Rubric | narrativerubric.pdf |
| 178 | Persuasive Writing Rubric | persuasiverubric.pdf |
| 179 | Descriptive Writing Rubric | descriptrubric.pdf |
| 180 | Informational/Explanatory Writing Rubric | explanarubric.pdf |
| 181 | Quarter-Pound Hamburgers | exemplar1.pdf |
| 182 | Tips and Wages | exemplar2.pdf |
| 183 | Running Ruben | exemplar3.pdf |
| 184 | Licorice | exemplar4.pdf |
| 185 | Buddy's Play Area | exemplar5.pdf |
| 186 | Picking Oranges with Bill and Frank | exemplar6.pdf |

# Contents of the Digital Resource CD *(cont.)*

| Title | Filename |
|---|---|
| A New Sled | modeltext.pdf |
| Scientific Conclusion | mentortext1.pdf |
| Acute and Obtuse Angles | mentortext2.pdf |
| Letter 1 | mentortext3.pdf |
| Letter 2 | mentortext4.pdf |
| Homework | mentortext5.pdf |
| A Mathematician Comes to Know an Orange | mentortext6.pdf |
| Ratio | mentortext7.pdf |
| Soccer Paragraph Frame | soccerframe2.pdf<br>soccerframe3.pdf<br>soccerframe4.pdf |
| Novels Paragraph Frame | novelsframe2.pdf<br>novelsframe3.pdf<br>novelsframe4.pdf |
| Bowling Paragraph Frame | bowlingframe2.pdf<br>bowlingframe3.pdf<br>bowlingframe4.pdf |
| Zoo Tickets Paragraph Frame | zooticketsframe2.pdf<br>zooticketsframe3.pdf<br>zooticketsframe4.pdf |
| Tips Paragraph Frame | tipsframe2.pdf<br>tipsframe3.pdf<br>tipsframe4.pdf |
| Tires Paragraph Frame | tiresframe2.pdf<br>tiresframe3.pdf<br>tiresframe4.pdf |
| One-Step Problems (Number Model) | onestepnumbermodel.pdf |
| Two-Step Problems (Number Model) | twostepnumbermodel.pdf |

# Notes